My Light
at the
End
of the
Tunnel

Enjoy!
Helen Bowers

MY LIGHT
AT THE
END
OF THE
TUNNEL

*The journey from abandoned child
and abused wife to a loved woman.*

BY HELEN BOWERS
AS TOLD TO FAY CHOBAN

Expert Publishing, Inc.
Andover, Minnesota

Photograph Credits:
  School Main Building—Fay Choban
  Coat Magazine Ad—Magazine Ad from Orphanage records
  Mr. and Mrs. Nick Choban—*Minneapolis Morning Tribune*
  Helen, Age 18—Helen Bowers
  Helen and Hansel—Helen Bowers
  Helen and Ed 1986—Mary Ellen Hernandez
  Young Children—Helen Bowers
  Barb, Bob, Mitch and Bette—Olan Mills Photography
  State School Kids monument—Fay Choban
  Helen and Ed, 2005—Fay Choban

ISBN-10: 1-931945-32-2
ISBN-13: 978-1-931945-32-5

Library of Congress Catalog Number: 2005932624

Printed in the United States of America

First Printing: September 2005

08 07 06 05   6 5 4 3 2 1

Expert Publishing, Inc.
14314 Thrush Street NW
Andover, MN 55304-3330
1-877-755-4966
www.ExpertPublishingInc.com

Dedicated

To

Ed Bowers, my husband,
the constant light in my life

and

Fay Choban, my daughter-in-law, because
without her there would be no book

and

The orphans at The State Public School for
Dependent and Neglected Children
Owatonna, Minnesota from 1886-1945

TABLE OF CONTENTS

ACKNOWLEDGEMENTS FROM HELEN BOWERS

I am blessed to have many wonderful friends. The encouragement all of you gave me helped make this book possible. I would especially like to thank Dawn and Jerry Fish, Kathleen Laughlin, Harvey and Maxine Ronglien, and Judy Skeie Voss for their help and ideas for the book.

ACKNOWLEDGEMENTS FROM FAY CHOBAN

Thank you, Bob, my wonderful husband, for all of the support, encouragement, and ideas you gave me throughout the whole book writing process. Your faith in my ability to do this kept me going. You also provided me with one great mother-in-law.

This book never would have happened without my good friends in the Real Power Network. The books many of you have written inspired me to have faith in myself. You also made me accountable by getting me to actually say I was going to write this book. A special thank you to Sharron Stockhausen, also a Network member, because without my confidence in you and your publishing business, I would not have known what to do with the book after I wrote it.

INTRODUCTION FROM HELEN BOWERS

This is my true life story. The journey starts with Helen Hoover, a twice abandoned child who grows up in an orphanage. My life changes when I marry and become Helen Choban, the verbally and physically abused young wife and mother of four children. The last part of my story continues on with my life as Helen Bowers, the mature happy woman who looks back over eighty-plus years of my life.

I was born to parents who could not take care of me, did not love me, and did not want me. I spent my early life in an orphanage where I learned not to cry and what it was like to never hear anyone tell me "I love you." I remember my life as the bad times or the years when I felt like I was trapped in a dark tunnel, where I had no hope or happiness, and then finally the good times when life was bright and I felt loved. I overcame an early life of being abandoned, unloved; survived a marriage of verbal and physical abuse; dealt with the serious health problems of my children; struggled with my own bouts of deep depression, illness, and the other harsh realities of life to emerge finally a loving, happy adult.

People have asked me why I wanted to write this book. I felt it was important to share the power of the word love and to show and tell your children, family, and friends that you love them. You need to believe that no matter what happens to you in your life, you can overcome it if you believe in yourself and a higher power. I have tried to put the past behind me, but my past did shape my future. I could have let my experiences break me, but instead I became strong. You should not give up. My story may make you cry with sadness or smile with happiness, but most of all I hope it gives you courage and hope to go on and create a happy life for yourself.

INTRODUCTION FROM THE INTERVIEWER, FAY CHOBAN

For many years I have heard bits and pieces of Helen's life and the hardships she had to deal with. Helen said she wanted to share her story, and I knew we would be able to work together, so I said, "Let's stop talking about writing a book and get busy creating it." I have wanted to be a writer since I was a small child. Here was my chance to fulfill one of my dreams.

I knew I was ready for a new adventure. I have technical skills that would make writing and marketing a book possible, and I have people in my life that would inspire me and provide me with the skills I was missing. There was nothing to hold me back.

There were some problems I needed to solve to have the story make sense. There are three variations of dates and facts in Helen's story—what she remembered and thought was true about her family and being given away until she received her records, what she learned at about age seventy when she got her orphanage records, and what I discovered when I reviewed the orphanage records in detail and reconstructed a time line of events in her life. I wondered how I could write a book that incorporates these different circumstances. I also wanted a way for Helen to share her reflections on how past events in her life shaped who she has become, and, finally, I wanted to provide some historical perspective on events and people in the one-hundred-year time frame the book covers. My solution was to create a section called "Reflections and Information," and I've used it throughout the book to give you additional information.

THE MINNESOTA STATE PUBLIC SCHOOL FOR DEPENDENT AND NEGLECTED CHILDREN

The history of the school/orphanage where Helen was raised in Owatonna, Minnesota, is quite a story in itself. Between 1886 and 1945, almost sixty years, the State Public School for Dependent and Neglected Children, also called SPS and the Owatonna Orphanage, took in 10,635 children. *Webster's New World Dictionary* defines an orphanage as "an institution for orphans" and an orphan as "a child whose parents are dead." This institution had a broader definition of orphan. *The Children Remember* video tells us 56 percent of the children had both parents living, 39 percent had one parent still alive, and only the remaining 5 percent had both parents deceased. Helen and her brothers were part of the 56 percent who had both parents living. A visit to the orphanage museum in Owatonna or viewing their award winning documentary, *The Children Remember*, will tell you much more about the history of this institution and the children who grew up there.

We hope you enjoy our book.

THE
BEGINNING
1922–1930
HELEN AGE 1 TO 8

My parents were not prepared emotionally or financially to handle the responsibilities of a rapidly growing family. They were very poor, and by the time they had been married eleven years, they had five children. I was the third child and was born on October 7, 1922, in Waseca, Minnesota, to Harold Hoover and Fern Davidson. Waseca is a small town about seventy-five miles from Minneapolis, Minnesota. My parents would be gone for weeks at a time and leave my four brothers and me home alone. Someone, perhaps from our school, reported our situation to the authorities. I don't remember very much about these early days, but I do recall the day the social worker came out to our basement apartment and found us sitting on the floor eating raw potatoes. This was the only food in the apartment. The social worker took us from the apartment and put us in a private orphanage. That's when I entered a very dark tunnel, the tunnel where I would spend a good share of my life.

WARD OF THE STATE— 1930–1936

HELEN AGE 8–14

Orphanage records say that on April 3, 1930, my brothers and I were brought to United Charities in St. Paul, Minnesota. I have no memory of this happening. According to the records we were only there a short time before we were sent out to different places to live. At this time I was eight years old and my family consisted of two older brothers, Donald, age twelve and crippled in both legs by infantile paralysis (polio), and Harold, age eleven. My two younger brothers were Leslie, also called Jack, age seven, and Richard, also called Dick, age four. My mother's parents, who were living in South Dakota, said they would take my brother Jack. I have never been able to figure out their reasoning on this. I could see why they didn't want Donald because he was crippled. And if they wanted someone to work on their farm, then wouldn't they take Harold, who was older? If cuteness counted, then take the little one, Dick. Some things remain a mystery. Harold and Dick were sent to the Owatonna Orphanage and Donald went to Gillette Children's Hospital in St. Paul, Minnesota. I was sent to live with my uncle in Owatonna.

My first memories of this time are when I met this strange man who told me I should call him Uncle Harry. He was my father's brother. The records indicate there had been several discussions between my father and his brother and wife about them wanting me.

MEET HARRY AND LUCILLE

Before my uncle and his wife could become my foster parents, they had to be investigated and approved by a state social worker. The following information comes from a hand written investigation report, dated March 18, 1930, and gives insight into Harry [also called Dewey] and Lucille and what the social worker at the State School Orphanage considered important in a family environment. The report starts out with a description of where my aunt and uncle lived in Owatonna, Minnesota. It says that the general appearance of the house, which my aunt and uncle rented, was good; the eight-room home was in good condition; the house had very good furnishings; there was the presence of books and periodicals; the family occasionally would go to a Methodist church two and a half miles away; they lived one mile from a country school, two and one-half miles from town; and the school promised good education. Their reputation in the neighborhood was good.

"Mrs. Hoover [my uncle's wife] was formerly Miss Lucile [sic] Rose–who was assistant in Cottage Two for two years [a boy's cottage at the orphanage]. She was an excellent worker, absolutely clean, and very good to the boys. Mrs. Nicholson speaks highly of her. She has had a H.S. [High School] education and is a graduate of the State Teacher's College, Sioux City, Iowa, but she never taught school. Her parents, Mr. and Mrs. C.S. Rose, are farmers at Mitchell, Iowa. She has four sisters and three brothers—one sister, Mrs. H. R. Kemp, is on a farm at Mitchell, Iowa. Her two brothers are living with their parents. Mrs. Hoover is a fine housekeeper and an excellent mother to the three-month-old baby. She isn't nervous or excitable—takes things easy and is always calm and quiet. She is a good looking girl and takes good care of herself.

"Mr. Harry Hoover is a H. S. [High School] Graduate and also graduate of the Globe Business College in St. Paul. He was brought up by his uncle and aunt, Mr. and Mrs. W.D. Hoover, at Frederic, Wisconsin. His parents died when he and his brother, Harold, were quite young. [This is incorrect. Only his mother died when they were young.] Both were taken to Frederic and lived there and still does [sic]. Harry has been, for two years, in charge of selling the city papers brought down by truck. [Newspapers from the Twin Cities.] He arranges for their sale here [Owatonna] and also drives to Blooming Prairie and Austin twice a day with the city papers. This nets him on average of $100 a month. [This is equal to about $1080 a month in 2005 dollars]. He spends the rest of his time at other jobs—has worked in garages, etc. About March 1 they moved to a little farm, thirty a [acres], just south of town and hope [sic] to raise chickens—have a garden and make use of his [Harry's] spare time in a profitable manner. They have bought eighty-six hens, two cows, and a horse. In a week or so he will buy about five hundred little chicks—has a brooder house [place to raise chicks] and stove, etc. and is busy getting ready to the handle the job right. The house is in good condition—they have a nice yard—plenty of trees—apple trees—large strawberry patch and good garden space. Mr. Hoover is a good clean fellow—likes children—and is an energetic young man who seems to want to make use of all of his time.

"Mr. and Mrs. W. D. Hoover, paternal aunt and uncle, Frederic, Wisconsin, own a small farm there—they have a son at home and his father lives with them. [This was the couple that raised my father.] At present, Mr. and Mrs. Hoover [my parents] are working with a road gang. She [my mother] cooks and this keeps them away from home the greater part of the year, and it would not work well for a girl to be with them as they live in a tent wherever they happen to be working. Mrs. Hoover [my mother] wrote to Harry Hoover, [my uncle] asking him to take the little girl, Helen Hoover. The children's father has written asking Harry to take the girl. It seems that all the relations have looked to Harry as the one to take some of the children. Harry is willing and anxious to take Helen—his wife says if they had room she would take the whole family.

"I believe Helen will be given very good care in this home—Mrs. Hoover is anxious to get her so she will have company—as she doesn't like to be alone.

"I suggest that Helen be placed in this home and that Mrs. Gladys Woleal [state social worker], St. Paul, be notified and also that Harry Hoover be notified as he wants to drive up to St. Paul to get her.

Mayner Goodrick, State Agent"

This note was added to the report: *"Harry Hoover just received a letter signed by Harold Hoover, father of children committed. Address was Sioux Falls, S.D. He said it was better for the children to be placed in homes for adoption than to hold them for the mother."*

The state also did this investigation of Uncle Harry. I think the comments on alcohol use are particularly interesting. Prohibition was a law from 1920 until 1933. This was the content of the hand written report dated March 24, 1930.

"I visited Mrs. Burzinski with whom Harry and his wife roomed for one and one-half years. She speaks very well of them in every way. Says she never knew of Harry's drinking—never had any in her home and never knew him to have drank outside of the home. He always paid rent in advance—worked every day—never used rough language—didn't chew—and was a good steady fellow. He chummed with H.W. Loomis considerably for a while—against his wife's wishes—but quit before they left her home [Mrs. Burzinski's home]. Loomis was continually calling him up coaxing him down to the garage and off on trips with him.

"I visited Officers Harding and Black at the police station. Harding knows Harry well—says he's a fine worker, on the job 365 days a year and never heard a word against him in any way. Black said he had heard that Harry was perhaps bootlegging, but didn't believe it and paid no attention to it. Neither had ever heard or seen him take a drink.

"Harding says he will make some inquiries today and report to us in 24 hours if he hears anything definite about Harry's using liquor or handling it.

"All are of the opinion that the man is a fine fellow—steady as can be—a great worker—energetic and dependable and all believe the little girl Helen would have a good home with them."

I was only eight years old and did not know any of this was happening. All I knew was that my father had left us, my mother could not take care of us, and my brothers and I were all alone.

LIVING WITH UNCLE HARRY AND AUNT LUCILLE

Uncle Harry and Aunt Lucille lived in Owatonna, Minnesota, out in the country on a farm. He was twenty-seven and she was twenty-five. My uncle had a garden and some chickens, but he wasn't exactly a farmer. He worked delivering newspapers and twice a day he would bring them down from St. Paul, about sixty-five miles away, twice a day to the towns of Austin, Blooming Prairie, and smaller towns, like Owatonna. He would then load up the truck with bread and take it back to St. Paul. It seemed to me that he was always working.

My aunt had a new baby, Robert, to take care of, and so I was usually left on my own. I can remember being outside and running through all the beautiful tall pine trees surrounding the house. My toys were the usual things that girls had. I played with dolls, jacks, had a sandbox, and a tire swing. I remember one of my chores was to gather eggs from the chicken coop. I did have a problem when I went to get the eggs. I was scared of the chickens and when they came too close to me I would drop my egg pail and break the eggs. My aunt didn't like that very much.

I was eight when I was taken from my parents but I don't remember ever going to school and, based on the records from the State Agent, I think my brothers and I missed school quite a bit. At my uncle's I went to a country one-room schoolhouse. I remember walking to school carrying my books and a lunch box. I also know that it got really cold on those walks. One other memory is of getting into the school room in the winter and finding that our bucket of drinking water was frozen. The teacher would have to put it on the wood stove to thaw and then we had water to drink.

One very vivid memory was sitting with one of my girl friends up on hill by the orphanage playground. I would watch the children play softball and look for my brothers. I could see the girls who lived at the orphanage out playing and I would laugh at them for wearing long baggy dresses and black cotton knit stockings. Those clothes were so old fashioned and ugly. My life was so much better than theirs. I was free to do what I wanted, and they were restricted and always had adults watching them. This would come back to haunt me.

I was never a very feminine little girl. I never wanted any frills or bows on my clothes. My aunt was good to me, but not an especially ambitious woman. She made me work hard around the house. I learned very early how to cook, clean, and take care of a baby. I was a very loving child, but always on the giving end and seldom upon the receiving end.

After a year or so my aunt, uncle, cousin Robert, and I moved into the town of Owatonna. We lived right behind the grade school. My life was really beginning to look pretty good to me. I felt as if I was actually starting to be part of a family. My aunt's sister Jean lived in Rochester, Minnesota, about forty miles from Owatonna. These relatives had one son about my age and we would visit back and forth. It was nice to have someone to play with.

Uncle Harry was the coach of a city baseball team and I became the mascot, water girl, bat girl, and did any other job they gave me. I just loved to go with him to the games. My little cousin had bad lungs and was a very sickly boy so my aunt never took him to a game. I sort of took the place of my uncle's son and he sure took the place of my dad. I might have called him uncle, but in my heart he was everything I could have wanted in a father. Everything I did was for him, not my aunt.

I remember once I brought home a bad conduct slip from school. Back then that's what the school did if you were misbehaving, or, in my case, talking too much. My uncle was not happy about it, and he said I couldn't go to the game that night. I was really mad I could not go. I promptly told him I hoped he would break a leg sliding into a base. He came home after the game with his hand bandaged up. He broke two fingers sliding into second base. Instead of showing him

11

how bad I felt, I said, "I told you so." After that I went to all the games. I don't know if he was afraid of my power or if I started behaving better.

I got quite an education sitting in the back booth at Steve's Cigar Store, which was a bar, on Main Street. I was usually the only child in the bar and all the men were so nice to me. They would be drinking their beverages and would send over piles of potato chips and pop to me, and I would sit for hours listening while the players replayed the whole game.

My life was shattered on September 2, 1934. My uncle got killed while driving his truck back from Austin after delivering bread and papers. He was just a month short of his thirty-third birthday. I don't remember much about what happened except that there were three men sitting in the seat of the truck. I later learned my uncle had multiple fractures, a torn bladder, a paralyzed bowel, and other internal injuries. The other men in the accident were seriously injured. The person I loved the most, and the only person who I thought cared for me, was dead. I was devastated, not only because he was killed, but also because I thought I had caused it. This was not too long after I had told him I hoped he would break a leg. I hid in the closet and cried and would not come out. I did not go to the funeral. I refused to accept the fact that he was dead.

After Uncle Harry died we all moved to Rochester, about forty-five miles from Owatonna, where my aunt's sister Jean lived. My cousin Robert started treatment for his lung condition at the Mayo Clinic, and I started going to school there. I made one special girlfriend in this school and learned that she was from the orphanage and was working out in a doctor's home as a domestic. She would tell me stories about what went on the orphanage and what her life was like. I had gone up to the orphanage to see my brothers a few times while living in Owatonna, but it wasn't a happy place and not one I wanted to visit very often.

These times must have been very difficult for my aunt. She was a young widow with a very sick small child. His treatments at the Rochester Mayo Clinic were not helping his lungs and he was getting worse. She was advised to take him to the southern states like Arizona, New Mexico, or Texas. For some unknown reason my parents never legally released any of us to be adopted, so even though I had been living with them, I was still a ward of the state. I can remember Aunt Lucille taking me aside and saying, "Helen, I don't know how to tell you this, but Robert is sick and the doctors think he can get better if we move somewhere warmer. I have to move out of state and you can't come with us. You are still a ward of the state and can't leave. You will have to go to the orphanage, like your brothers did."

Aunt Lucille wrote the following letter to the orphanage on January 11, 1936.

"Dear Sir,

"I am writing you in regards to Helen Hoover, whom I have been keeping since 1930. Since my husband passed away a year ago last fall I have

13

made every effort to keep her, but find at this time that I cannot afford to keep her any longer.

"The doctors at the Mayo Clinic have advised me to take my little boy, who has a chest complication, to a dry climate, preferably Texas, and I may not return for several years. I am planning on leaving soon and find it financially impossible for me to take her along. Your agent Mr. Yaeger told me, after my husband's death, that at any time I felt I could no longer afford to keep her I could bring her to the school.

"Please advise me if I can bring her to you on Sunday, January 19. Since I cannot make definite plans for leaving until I have found a satisfactory place to leave her.

"Trusting to hear from you at your earliest convenience.

I am Sincerely, Mrs. Lucille Hoover"

My next home was going to be the orphanage. This was going to be hard a transition for me as I had been living a fairly free life with few restrictions. When I was making fun of the girls at the orphanage and their old fashioned clothes, little did I know I'd soon be one of them and wearing the same clothes as they did. I was so scared. I thought the other kids would beat me up and laugh at me. These kids would remember me as the girl who came to visit her brothers in the orphanage. They would remember that I laughed and made fun of them.

I never saw my Aunt Lucille or Robert again. She did write to me after she returned from the South and was again living in Rochester with her sister, and I talked to her once on the phone. She had remarried, but her new husband was not healthy and they were married only ten years before he died. She did have one daughter and was living in Rochester. Robert got married and moved to Colorado. I don't think he ever worked. His wife worked and supported him while he devoted his life to spreading his religious beliefs to others.

School Records About My Parents

Sometime after the Owatonna State School closed, its records were sent to the Minnesota Historical Society and they remained sealed there for many years. In the mid 1990s, when I was in my seventies, laws about opening those records changed, and I saw on the news that I could get them. I was curious and so I requested they be sent to me. The first thing that surprised me was how detailed they were. The second surprise was what I learned about my family, and I wished desperately that I had kept my curiosity to myself. The following is from the Owatonna Schools case worker's initial report. When they described the family character, habits, physical and mental conditions, it simply said, "Parents weak character" and then went on:

"Helen, Harold, and Richard Hoover, were brought to this school April 3, 1930, by Mrs. Elizabeth Lilly, United Charities' visitor, St. Paul. Helen did not remain at the school but was placed direct with paternal uncle, Harry Hoover, Steele

County, Owatonna, Minn., accompanied by Mrs. Lilly. Parents have a weak character. The mother is reported to have come from a family of several children none of whom made good. The father, whose parents died when he was young, made his home with relatives until going to Dakota where he met Fern Davidson whom he married. She had one illegitimate child (Donald) by a man who had worked for her father. Paternity has not been established. Both parents would go to dances, go to cafes for meals and attend theaters while the children were left at home alone with scarcely anything to eat. Their home was always upset—work left undone—mother was a poor housekeeper and would rather get away from home and have a good time than care for her children. She deserted her family on June 8, 1929, after which time the children were cared for at the Protestant Orphan Asylum, but father failed to pay for their board and they were committed to S.P.S. [State Public School]. Family was reported to the United Charities in 1929, as Mr. Hoover, who was working for the National Battery Co., was being garnished. Reports were received that the children were being neglected. Both parents would go to dances and leave the children alone. Mrs. Hoover was shiftless and a poor housekeeper. Children were absent from school a great deal of the time. On 6-8-29 Mrs. Hoover deserted the family and Mr. Hoover asked that the children be cared for. On 6-14-29 a petition was filed in juvenile court on the dependency and neglect of the children. On 6-2-29 Mr. Hoover was ordered by the court to pay $40.00 per month for the care of the children."

From state agent workers report dated March 18, 1930:

"Harry [my uncle] gave me a great deal of information about the relatives and parents of the five Hoover children [my parents, brothers, and myself]. Their father, Harold Hoover, never amounted to much. He was always borrowing money and never could support his family. He is only twenty-nine years old and perfectly able to work. When he has had jobs, he and his wife would spend the money foolishly, go to cafes for meals and attend theaters while the children were left at home with scarcely anything to eat. Her mother, Mrs. Tom Davidson, Sutton, N.D. is a good woman, but none of her children have amounted to anything. Harry says that one of the boys came here to visit him a year ago and he was nothing but a bum and a tramp. He wouldn't even have him visit their home or remain overnight. A daughter is married and lives in Minneapolis and she is the only decent one of the children. The Davidsons are not well off financially and Harry Hoover thinks the home is not a satisfactory place for any of these children."

I could not believe it when I read that my mother left us. All my life I believed my father left us; my mother worked several jobs, and was trying to hold our family together but just could not do it and so sent us away. The other very painful news was learning my "brother" Donald was not my full brother. He was an illegitimate son my mother had before she met my father. I felt that the description of my parents from the case workers was not flattering and it hurt me deeply. No matter how old you are you always want to believe the best about your parents.

REFLECTION AND INFORMATION ON MY PARENTS

I have often thought about what my life would have been like if Uncle Harry had not died. I would have grown up with people who loved and wanted me, celebrated birthdays, had nice clothes, probably have a different view of what a normal life should be and how I should be treated, and maybe even gotten an education. Perhaps I would have married when I was a little older and certainly I would have found a different husband. How different my life would have been, but I can't dwell on the past. That is not what happened.

I have been trying to understand what life was like for my parents in hopes that I might figure out why they gave us up. My father was born in 1898 in St. Paul, Minnesota. He had one brother, my Uncle Harry. His parents were farmers. My father's mother died when he was very small, and his father, Newt, took the two boys to live with his parents. Newt also lived with them in Frederic, Wisconsin. I think my father had about a third-grade education. He was epileptic and so, between the lack of education and seizures, the only work he could get was doing odd jobs whenever he could find them.

My mother, Fern Davidson, was born in Sutton, North Dakota, in 1900. At this time North Dakota had been a state only eleven years. Her family consisted of ten sisters and two brothers, and her parents were farmers. She only had a sixth-grade education and never worked outside the home. Over one hundred years later it is almost impossible for me to imagine how much of a frontier North Dakota was. She grew up in the Wild West!

I don't know what circumstances brought my father to North Dakota, where he met my mother. She already had one young illegitimate son, Donald, when they met. In 1919 you would think that the stigma of that child was quite a burden and Fern would have wanted to leave. They were then married on September 19, 1919, and two months later my brother Harold was born. World War I had just ended and the war time economic boom was over. The eighteenth amendment was ratified which started prohibition, and it was the start of the "Roaring 20s." My father was twenty-one and my mother was nineteen. She came from a very rural area and coming to the "big city" of St. Paul must have been quite an experience.

I imagine this young couple with two children had a difficult life. They lived back and forth between St. Paul, Minnesota, and Frederic, Wisconsin, about seventy miles apart.

When my father could find work, they lived in St. Paul, but when there was no work or food we would move back to live with his aunt and uncle in Frederic. My mother did not work. She had her hands full taking care of all of us kids. She had given birth to at least six children by the time she was thirty. Money was scarce and what little they had, the records indicate they spent on going out and doing fun things. I would think they felt overwhelmed by the circumstances of their life.

My parents' life was typical for the times. Birth rates in the early 1900s were much higher than today. Women between thirty-five and forty-nine had an average of 5.3 children. There were many diseases such as tuberculosis, typhoid fever, and diphtheria. Forty percent of the mothers experienced the death of a child. More than 100,000 people were described as roomers, boarders, and lodgers.

When I met my mother later on in my life, she was still a very fun loving person, so I don't find it hard to imagine that when she left us in early June 1929, when she was about thirty, she must have felt very trapped and unhappy. The great Black Monday stock market crash came on October 29, 1929, and I think that what little work my father had been able to find ended. By March 1930, he could no longer afford the forty dollars a month to keep the five of us at United Charities Home. This would be equal to about $432 in 2005 dollars. He had no wife, no money, and had run out of other options, so he was forced to give us up to the orphanage or to relatives.

THE
SCHOOL
1936–1940
HELEN AGE 14 TO 18

MY FIRST DAY

When I was fourteen years old I found that I had become one of those girls in a baggy dress and black cotton stockings that I had laughed at. Not a pleasant outlook for me. I will never forget my first day at Cottage

School Main Building

Twelve when I was standing in front of the big window looking out over the snow covered hill and thinking how alone I was. The tears started to come and just then I turned around and was slapped very hard across the face by an assistant matron and told, "We don't allow crying here. You are here because nobody wants you, and we don't want you either but we are stuck with you." These words have stuck in my mind ever since. I was not wanted or loved by anyone.

THE COTTAGES

Cottage Twelve was better known as Detention Cottage. This was the only cottage that housed both boys and girls from ages three to sixteen. When you arrived here they checked you for head lice, fleas, and every other possible disease you could have. To get rid of the head lice they would wash your hair with gasoline. The physical exams were very embarrassing for a young teenage girl. Every time you left the school and came back you would have to go back to the Detention Cottage and go through all these checkups. This was not something you wanted to repeat very often. Children would stay in Cottage Twelve until there was room for them in another cottage. For me, after three weeks I was moved to Cottage Thirteen. This cottage had an average of twenty-four girls, ages six to thirteen. It was staffed with a head matron and two assistants. The head matron lived on the premises in an apartment. Her job was to keep an eye on us and our belongings and manage the assistants. The assistants lived off the premises. They were responsible for discipline, of which there was plenty;

assigning us our chores; making us keep the cottage clean; seeing that we got to meals and did our school work. The cottages had a very nice living room which was upstairs and we spent many an hour polishing those wood floors on our hands and knees. This was the room that visitors saw, but we were never allowed upstairs in the living room, except for special occasions.

It did not take me very long before I had another experience with discipline, and it was quite a dramatic one. On my first day in Cottage Thirteen I was told some of the rules, and one rule was that words as gosh, golly, and darn were always swear words. Having been raised in a normal home these words were part of my vocabulary. Right off, I said, "Gosh, what can you say?" Immediately hands went up informing the assistant matron what I had said. The rule was that you had to raise your hand and be recognized before you could speak. I received ten very hard slaps on both sides of my face. I sat down and incredibly said, "Gee, can't you say anything?" Once again the girls hands go up and I got twenty more slaps. By this time my face was beginning to turn red and swell. The assistant decided I'd better go up and see the head matron. The matron told me how hard it was going to be to adhere to all the rules but said that this punishment should not have happened. This matron showed me the only kindness I had seen yet. I soon learned not to say anything unless I was spoken to. My personality changed from that of a happy extrovert to an unhappy introvert.

The discipline was strict, my activities were more restricted, and my life was different from what it had been, but staying at the school wasn't really all that bad for me. I had a clean bed to sleep in and three meals a day which was more than I had living with my parents. The hardest part was that I did not know where my parents were or why they left me. Children can be very cruel and they would say things like "Your mother must really hate you because she doesn't come to see you or write to you." I wanted a mother so bad. I'd have taken anyone on the street if only they would have let me call them mother. To have a mother who would tuck me in at night and tell me "I love you" was something I dreamed about, but it never happened.

DAILY LIFE IN THE ORPHANAGE

Our special place was our chair. All of the children had their own chairs in a room in the basement of our cottage, which was a playroom. These chairs were our life, our home base. If I was not outside playing or doing my chores, I sat on my chair. I sat with my hands folded and did not talk or slump. I was not allowed to talk but I could read, unless I was being punished. This was also where I kept my few private belongings. There was a little cloth bag, about twelve inches square, that hung on the back of the chair. I might keep a comb, maybe a hair ribbon or a few coins in the bag. Other than that my only other storage was one dresser drawer in the cottage. I remember spending a lot of our time sitting on these chairs. Can you imagine our children today sitting quietly on a chair for hours or having all their clothes, toys, and books in one drawer?

There were many more rules for me to get used to. I lived in constant fear of doing the wrong thing, no matter how small it might be, and this is when I started to wet the bed. When I wet the bed I would have to sit all day in my chair. I was always supposed to do what I was told immediately, and I never talked back because if I did I was punished. Slapping on the face was common as was having the radiator brush hit my leg or butt. If a matron asked me to do something and I did not move as fast she thought I should, she would punish me. A common punishment was for her to put a broomstick across the seat of a chair and then with my face toward the back of the chair kneel on the broom stick for three or more hours. When I got off I couldn't walk. If I was caught talking I spent the rest of the day in silence, and I liked to talk.

We went up for bed at 9:00 P.M. We were supposed to kneel by the bed and say our prayers until the matron had checked to see that everyone in the cottage was ready for bed. The matron would start the bedtime routine on the floor where the smallest children were and work her way up to our bedroom. This would usually take at least an hour. By this time my head was on my bed and I was asleep. All of a sudden I would feel my hair being pulled and I'd start the "Our father who art in heaven" prayer faster than it's ever been said. More then once I would have to kneel and say that prayer for several hours more. The matron would check back on me, and the other girls, to make sure we were all still doing our prayer punishment. I think the boys faced even harsher punishment.

Special occasions were few and far between. I knew when Easter came because I got a newer set of clothes and for Christmas I might get a little more food. Thanks to the Kiwanis Clubs there was a piece of fruit by each child's plate on Christmas. I don't think many children ate their fruit. I know I saved it as long as I could and by that time it usually spoiled. I can remember getting an empty perfume bottle for doing extra work for the matron and putting a little water in the bottle so it would smell good. I would also celebrate the Fourth of July by playing softball. I don't remember ever seeing a parade or fireworks. As for birthdays, many of the children had no idea how old they really were, much less what day they were born, so there was never a birthday party. I can't help but think how different this is from today's world. Parents and friends have so many opportunities now to make children feel special, but I wonder how much of the celebration is taken for granted.

I don't remember having much free time. Keeping kids busy kept us out of mischief, but there were fun times at the orphanage, especially when I participated in a special event. At times like this I would see a light in the tunnel. I sang in the choir so I got to be in some of the plays and concerts. These were given for the people of Owatonna. My only other contact with the town people was when we would go downtown on Saturday night and listen to the band playing in Central Park. My father left me with a little money when I was brought to the orphanage, and I earned more from cleaning the matron's rooms or watching the little kids in the dining room, so I had a few pennies to spend on candy. You can't imagine what a treat this was. I was active in sports such as tennis and softball. The orphanage even had an indoor swimming pool.

The school had a music department, and a couple times a year the better singers would be picked to perform in oper-ettas at the Faribault School for the Feeble Minded and Blind and in town. I loved doing this. When polishing floors or feeling sad, we sang this song:

> I am a little orphan girl.
> My mother, she is dead.
> My father is a poor man
> Who cannot buy no bread.
> I sit by the fire and hear the organs play.
> It sounds like my mother's, but she is far away.
> Far Far off in heaven where no one can see.
> Far Far off in heaven where no one can tell.

Our dresses were made at Shakopee, Minnesota, about sixty miles away, where there was a detention center for unwed mothers. I got the same clothes those girls wore, they were not uniforms, they were maternity dresses. I tried my best to make these clothes stylish and would use belts to gather in the dresses to make them fit me better. I had three outfits. One was for Sunday and special occasions, one for school, and one for play. Almost always the clothes were hand me downs from an older girl. Maybe she outgrew her Sunday dress so then it became my Sunday dress. When it got looking a little worn it became a school dress and when it was patched and had holes it was the play dress. One of the school rules was that we had to wear hats to church. There was a matron who would go St. Paul to buy the hats. She seemed to me to be about eighty years old, so you can guess what they looked like. I remember I had one that was styled like a man's hat, but I didn't know any different so I thought it was great. I learned to sew when I was fourteen years old and then I could make my own clothes. One of my first sewing projects was to make a house coat with bound buttons. I was so proud of myself because no one else had a house coat.

Later on, when I was working in homes, I desperately wanted a store bought coat that I saw in a magazine advertisement. I asked my case worker about it and she said no because there was no money for it, so I wrote this letter to the case supervisor, Mr. Doleman, in early August 1940.

"Dear Sir:

"I am writing this at the request of Miss McConnville. I would like very much to have a winter coat made as nearly like the enclosed picture. If no great inconvenience, could I possibly have a dark green fabric or camel's hair cloth? I'd be very grateful.

Coat Magazine Ad

"My measurements are as follows:

Bust: 34 inches
Waist: 26 inches

Hip: 35 inches
Sleeve: 24 ½ inches
Neck: 15 inches
Length: 41 inches

"Will appreciate anything you can do for me.

"Sincerely, Helen Hoover"

I received this reply back from him.

"Dear Helen:

We will have to supply your coat out of the stock secured by the State School by the state. I believe you will have the most satisfaction out of having Miss McConville select your coat from the stock so that it will be as near as possible to the approximate size and design you have suggested in your letter. I will refer this letter to Miss McConville when she returns.

Very truly yours,

George H. Doleman, Case Supervisor"

I did get a coat that was close to what I wanted and, at age seventeen, I finally had my very first store bought coat. Even today I am surprised that I wrote the letter and that they seemed to take it seriously. They had the magazine ad in my file. The orphanage might not give us love, but they did really try to take care of us in the best way they could.

The orphanage was self sufficient. All of this took much work to maintain so there was plenty for the children to do.

We did chores like make bread, take care of the livestock, tend the many gardens where the vegetables and fruit were grown, worked in the canning facilities, laundry, hospital, and baby nursery. Each cottage did specific kinds of work. For example the boys in one cottage would take care of a huge garden. The boys in another cottage would take care of the animals, do lawn maintenance, or work in the laundry. The best job that a girl could get was working in the baby nursery. After that it was working as a maid in the superintendent's home or waiting tables in the matron's dining room. These last two were special because you got much better food. If I was assigned to clean the matron's room, I might get a nickel as extra money. It was also good to be assigned to take care of the smaller children at meal times. For example, there were three small tables where little boys ages one to three ate. If I was chosen to take care of the children at the three tables, their matron gave me a nickel every Friday night. Everyone wanted this job. The only problem was when one of them cried or got out of hand the matron would tap the bell and say, "Helen, if you can't handle the children, maybe you should sit in their seat." In front of three hundred children, this is not what I needed to hear. I can't remember ever being praised for what I did, and yet I was one of the better behaved girls. Most girls worked in the kitchen or did cleaning.

Our meals weren't bad by my standards. We had many meals of soups, stews, and boiled dinners. I learned how to can. All of our meals had to be cooked in big vats or kettles. Cooking for three hundred children wasn't easy. We had no fried foods at all. I never knew what fried potatoes or fried meat was until I was out in a working home. Sunday was the special day. I had corn flakes for breakfast and boiled liver and gravy and mashed potatoes and peas for dinner. This was a real treat. We did have a good bakery and always had a plentiful supply of fresh bread, cakes, and cookies. Boys in the orphanage were the bakers. My two brothers worked in the bakery.

The orphanage kept good records of our lives. I think this was quite an accomplishment given everything was done on paper with a typewriter for thousands of children during the years the orphanage existed. I was surprised to see records indicating my father wrote to me in June of 1937 and my mother visited me in July of 1937. They have detailed records of my grades, and regular reports on my behavior. Here are some examples of the twenty-one questions that they used to evaluate us:

> *Is he/she easy to manage or does he/she make trouble?*
>
> *Is he/she accepted by the other children?*
>
> *What is his/her reaction to group play?*
>
> *Does he/she tattle on others?*

The records indicate I was an average student with an IQ of 103 and most of the time got along well with others. Here is one description of me:

> "Helen is a good worker. Does not resent correction and does as she is told. She is very active, mixes with all the children, likes group play, sort

31

of acts as a leader. She is very clean and neat about herself and jolly most of the time. Likes to read and entertain herself. Is very active in sports, as tennis, swimming, and kitten ball and is interested in scout [Girl Scout] work."

I always thought of myself as being small, but orphanage records indicate at fourteen I was five feet tall and eighty-eight pounds and by age seventeen I was five feet two inches tall and one hundred and twenty-one pounds. I think this was pretty average for the time.

REFLECTION AND INFORMATION ON ORPHANAGE LIFE

While we were in the orphanage my father came to see my brothers and me once. When I was told he was in the visitors' room I didn't want to go until my brothers went. I was afraid that there might be two men in the room, and I wouldn't know which one was my father.

My mother also came once and brought me a red satin blouse. What did she think an orphan would do with a red satin blouse? That's my mother.

The school did not want you to build any relationships with your siblings, so they kept us apart. I could only see one brother once a month for an hour. One reason for this was because then there was not much chance of siblings planning a breakaway together. My brothers hated the orphanage and tried to run away more than once. The orphanage wanted us to adjust to our life at the school and did not want siblings to start thinking and talking about their life before the orphanage.

I have four years which are completely lost to me. It was not until writing this book and looking closely at the orphanage records that my daughter-in-law put together all the pieces of my age at various times and figured out when things really happened. She knew my story and the ages I had always given her and they just did not match up. She had to convince me my life was not as I remembered. I did not believe her at first. I thought I lived with my uncle from ages four to eight and went to the orphanage when I was about eight. In reality, I was with my aunt and uncle from ages eight to fourteen. I also thought my brothers were all four years younger than they were when we had been abandoned. I will tell you more about the reason for this lapse in memory later on in my story.

In addition to the four lost years, I have almost no memory of my early years with my parents, up until about age eight when I went to live with Uncle Harry. One of my brothers told me that after I was born my parents made my bed in a shoe box and then a dresser drawer. I don't remember where we lived, going to school, playing with children, any holiday events or birthday parties. I did not know until I turned eighteen that I had one other sibling who died very young. All my life I have purposely put that baby or small child out of my mind. I don't know what its name was or how long it lived or how it died. I am really not very interested in knowing about what happened.

A few of the things that I learned at the orphanage carried over into my adult life. My kids tell me their memories of a mother who was a perfectionist and made them polish floors, just like she had to, and cooked boiled dinners for them. They still hate boiled dinners. If you don't know what a boiled dinner is, it is a ham hock, potatoes, onions, cabbage, carrots, and rutabaga all boiled together. Those teenage years wearing embarrassing, homemade, hand me down clothes made a lasting impact on me. I so looked forward to the time when I could wear store bought, pretty clothes and to this day a new outfit always seems to cheer me up.

WORKING IN HOMES

Your only future at the orphanage was to get an education and go out to a working home. If you did not go to school or work out in a home, your prospects of getting out of the orphanage were slim. Many children ended up spending their whole life in the orphanage, first as an orphan and later as a paid employee. The laundry was one place the school especially needed skilled workers and permanent employees. It was dangerous work and hard to teach children what to do. You went out to work when you were about fifteen. The boys usually went out to a farm or found a job in a factory. The owner of the power plant in Owatonna gave many of the boys jobs.

Having an education was a value that my aunt and uncle had. She was a high school graduate and a graduate of a state teacher's college and he was a high school graduate and a graduate of Globe Business College. That was quite a bit of education for this time in history. They impressed on me that the only way to get ahead was to get my high school degree. This is why education was very important to me. My only request when placed in a home was that I was allowed to go to school. I knew that I had to keep a B average, but I could do it if I was given the chance.

When in the homes I would do all I was told and get paid $1.00 a week. If you convert that into 2005 dollars, that is about $13 a week. My clothing and school supplies were paid for by the State School. I would do just about anything to stay in the home because if I was taken back to the orphanage I would have to go through Detention Cottage again. Also, the other kids would give you a hard time if you came back. They would say you were really no good and worthless if you couldn't even work in a home.

My first working home was in Owatonna, Minnesota. I had to take care of a newborn baby and a boy just a year younger than myself. I was about fifteen. My first night at the home I had to do the dishes left after a big party and take care of the baby. I received no instructions and I was scared to death because I never had this much responsibility and the baby was only two weeks old. I was so afraid I would do something wrong and be punished. The boy took pride in beating me on the back with a belt just to see me cry. His mother would come over and I would tell her what happened and she would say, "Well, if he hit you he must have had a good reason. What did you do to him?" This went on for several months until one day I went to school and the teacher saw that I was bleeding through my blouse. I told them what happened and they called my social worker and I was taken back to the orphanage. I was at that home from August 1937 until March of 1938.

After I was taken out of my first home I was allowed to work for the Orphanage Superintendent, Mr. Velve. I worked as a maid and waited on tables in his home. This was great as I got to eat the leftovers. They had food I hadn't eaten in a long time, things like pork chops, fried potatoes, and all the good stuff. I worked there for almost six months.

My next home was with the Hertz family. They were Jewish and lived in St. Paul. They had a three-year-old girl, Sandra. I had my own room and the people were very nice. I remember when I first got there Mrs. Hertz told me they were having company, and I needed to make a roast and a chocolate cake. I forgot the cake in the oven and when I took it out it was about one inch high. Mr. Hertz was so nice. He said I should just put some frosting on it, and when they served it to company, he commented on how good my brownies were. Anyone else would have punished me. They also made sure that I had a Christmas tree in my room. Another time they left for the evening, and I had some boy and girl friends over, which I should not have done. When they came back home my friends were still there. Mr. Hertz politely introduced himself and said it was getting late and it was time for my friends to leave. Afterward I got scolded, but he did not do it in front of my friends. Mr. Hertz had a brother who had a business selling women's dresses. He traveled quite a bit and sometimes came to stay with us for four or five days. When that happened the brother got my bed and I had to sleep on a cot in the porch but that was ok with me because when he left I would get a dress or two to keep. I had real clothes.

My life as a teenager might seem unusual to you, but I knew nothing different. I wrote the following letter to my girlfriends back at the orphanage while I was at the Hertz home. I think I sound like a pretty normal sixteen-year-old girl who is interested in boys, movies, and clothes.

"Dear girls, and everybody,

"I'm so sorry I didn't write sooner, but I've been so very busy. I will start out by telling you how much I miss you and end up by telling you the same thing, but in between I'll tell you about my home.

"The people's name is Hertz. They are the grandest people you could ever work for. I get $1.00 a week [during the summer], $1.50 a week on school days. [I got an extra fifty cents to cover my transportation.] I get $ .25 for mowing the lawn. The work here is very simple. There are only three in the family. Mr. and Mrs. Hertz and Sandra, their little girl. She [Sandra] has long curls down to her shoulders. Her hair is just beautiful. Mr. and Mrs. have natural wavy hair too. I'm going to get a permanent the week before school starts. I can have one now if I want it. But I think I will wait.

"I didn't miss out of seeing the show 'Joy of Living' I saw it last night at the Grandview Theater. It is about five blocks from our house. I saw

'Vicious Lady' with Ginger Rogers on Sunday. I have all day Sunday and every Thursday afternoon off. Donald [my brother] took me to the show Sunday afternoon.

"I played a couple matches of tennis. I play with Mrs. Hertz's brother. He's about twenty and a lot better player, but we have loads of fun. There aren't hardly any girls around here. But plenty of boys that I don't like very well. I have a lot of fun with our dog, Pal. He's the cutest thing.

"I might go to Chicago next week or some time in September and stay for two weeks. I will stay with Corrine. She is some relation to Mrs. Hertz. She is very cute. Fritze and Tom, Dick and Harry are about the only kids that I know in Chicago. They are all some relation to Mrs. Hertz. She is a dear to me.

"I've gotten two new dresses for fall. One is a green silk with lace collar and pockets. The other is a blue checked with a red zipper all the way down the front of it. It is just darling. I got a cute brown sailor hat for my winter coat. I'm getting a pair of blue shoes with the thick rubber soles for high school.

"I'll go to Central high school. I'll have a long way to go to school, but I won't mind. Their little girl is fine and in first grade. She is so very smart. She talks just like a grown up. I love her so.

"Now I'll finish by telling you how much I miss you kids. I get so lonesome and miss all the ball games. Who is captain of my side now? Who won the last game? Who umped? Do you still play tennis? With whom? Enough questions until next time. One thing I have to know is who is table waiter in my place? Now, I'll quit asking questions. Say hello to all the little girls for me, especially Peggy. Now, Helen, just because this is addressed to you don't be selfish and let the other girls and everyone look and read it. Ho Ho. As if they would want to.

Loads of love, Helen."

I didn't get in trouble for this letter, but I sure did with another one I wrote. I wanted to have the girls think I had boyfriends, so I wrote about all the boys I was seeing and kissing. The school opened all the mail we got and saw my letter and called me in for a talk. They wanted to know if I was having sex or making out. Of course, I didn't even know what that was. They tried to keep a close watch on us.

I went to school in the morning and spent the rest of my time watching Sandra, doing the cleaning, washing, ironing, and helping with the cooking. By this time I was sixteen and very capable. I lived there for one year and got along fine. The boy who lived next door went to a military academy and he invited me to their military ball. I was so excited. Mrs. Hertz had a sister who was my size and she was going to lend me one of her formals to wear to the dance. Unfortunately, my state worker came for a visit when I was trying on the dress. I told her I had been invited to the dance. The social worker told me I couldn't go and said to me, "You are not good enough to do this. You will forget who you are and think you are like normal people." They never let you forget who you are. Mrs. Hertz tried her best to explain things, but the social worker took me back to the orphanage using the excuse I had to have my tonsils out. I liked this home so much and having to leave seemed so unfair. I just wanted to be like the other girls in school and this home gave me the opportunity to have an almost normal teenage life. I was out of the tunnel when I lived with them. I was a real person. I was there from August 1938 to July 1939.

As it got closer to the next school year, I still didn't have a working home to go to. I remember I was walking across the orphanage lawn and one of the matrons came up to me and said, "I'm so glad you are going to be our new librarian." I didn't know what she was talking about and barged into the superintendent's office. This was absolutely not permitted. You were supposed to knock and wait to enter. He made me leave and come back in properly. I asked him why I wasn't going out to a home and continuing with school. He had promised me that I could go to school and I really wanted to. The orphanage's view was that I had too much freedom in the city and was becoming too independent. In other words, the last home treated me like a real person, so they did not want me to go out again. Their plans for me were that I would stay at the school and learn how to work in the library. I didn't care if I went to the big city. I told them they could even put me on a farm, but please put me in a home where I can finish my education.

When September 30 came, they put me out to another home in St. Paul. I would be going to a different high school, but I knew I could handle the schoolwork. This home was exactly what the orphanage wanted for their children. In the interviews they had with the family they probably determined that this place would provide me structure and the family would be strict with me. The man was so nice, but his wife was one of the most unloving and unreasonable people that I have ever met, and her treatment of me sent me back into the tunnel. There would be no light for me in this home.

This family had a newborn son and a two-year-old son. I had to do all the housework, cooking, wash the baby clothes by hand, stay up at night to give the baby his 10:00 P.M. bottle, and be up at 5:00 A.M. to get the husband's breakfast, while the wife slept in. The mother would see me nodding off at night as I fed the baby, but she would not help. It is surprising that I did not drop the baby. I think she resented me going to school and kept me as busy as possible so I had very little time for doing my homework. I got Thursday afternoon and Sunday afternoon off and could do what I wanted, but she had her husband watch me to see where I went so she could report back to the state agent.

They would always have a late dinner on Friday night so I was cooking and cleaning up later than usual. I was allowed to go out on Friday but because they were eating late I might not have all my kitchen work done. When my dates would come to pick me up she would say, "Helen isn't through with her work yet. You know she is the maid here." This always made a great impression on a seventeen-year-old boy.

By now I was starting to get tired of this treatment. I had a date on New Year's Eve to go roller skating. We left at 10:00 P.M. and I was told I had to be home by midnight. We did not have a car and had to go by street car the five miles to the roller rink so the timing was impossible to work out. When we went out the door my date said, "How are we going to make it home on time?" and I said, "We aren't." I got home at 1:00 A.M. and the state worker was waiting at the door. After this, things got even worse. For the next few months my privileges were restricted and there was a lot of friction between me and the lady of the house. Finally the lady of the house told me our arrangement was not going to work out and she was sending me back to the orphanage. I stayed in this home for six months from October 1939 to March 1940.

The last thing I wanted was to go back to the orphanage, and I was not alone in feeling this way. Two weeks earlier one of my girlfriends at the orphanage had been taken out of a working home and was going to be brought back to the orphanage. She could not bear the thought of this. The teasing from the other kids and going through Detention Cottage physical exams again were more than she could stand. Near Faribault, Minnesota, she jumped out of the car and was killed. I told my case worker I would do the same thing if they tried to send me back to the orphanage.

It is now March of 1940 and I was only about six months away from my eighteenth birthday, when I would no longer be a ward of the state, and it was my senior year in high school. The Hertz family I had worked for earlier agreed to take me back again until I could leave the orphanage for good. As important as an education had been to me, it now took second place to working for this family and staying out of the orphanage. So with only a few months to go, I never returned to finish my senior year. I also had a boyfriend and was thinking of marriage. I couldn't wait until I turned to be of age and no longer was a ward of the state of Minnesota. Little did I know what life had in store for me.

REFLECTION ON WORKING HOMES AND ORPHAN AND ABANDONED CHILDREN TODAY

My first working home family taught me how to take orders and what it felt like to be treated cruelly, taken advantage of, beaten, not believed or trusted. My second family appreciated the work I did for them. Even though they were strict, they showed me the most kindness I had seen in years. My third family taught me what it was like to be humiliated and unappreciated. I don't think I have ever met anyone who was as cruel as the woman in that home. Having learned these lessons has made me be a better person. I never want to treat people in the disrespectful way I was treated in that last home.

I don't think there is one best solution on how to take care of children such as my brothers and me. Adoption and foster homes certainly help in many ways. Another option even today is having children go to a place something like the cottages I grew up in. Mary Jo Copeland, here in the Twin Cities, Minnesota, is a wonderful example of someone who is making a positive difference in the lives of many people. She is the founder of Sharing and Caring Hands program. One of the projects she is working on is the Gift of Mary Children's Home, a group residential facility.

> The mission of Gift of Mary Children's Home is to provide a safe and loving, nurturing environment for children where they can grow emotionally, physically, spiritually, and academically, toward the goal of being happy, well adjusted, self-sufficient, responsible adults.

> The Gift of Mary Children's Home will offer education, vocation, social, recreational, and spiritual needs for children to develop and succeed in the future. This stable, long-term placement will keep siblings together to build a place that would provide a supportive addition to foster care for large sibling groups and those who are not being served in the current foster care system.

Her dreams face many challenges but her faith and persistence have helped her accomplish some incredible things.

A Brief History
of the Owatonna
State School

It is easy for us to look at our society now and how we take care of abandoned children and make judgments about the life I have described in the orphanage. What is more difficult to do is look back over 120 years to when the orphanage was started and understand what the current thinking was about how to best take care of orphan children. This orphanage during its lifetime provided a home to over 10,000 children. Fifty-six percent had both parents living, 39 percent had one parent still alive, and only the remaining 5 percent had both parents deceased.

The following brief history and philosophy of the orphanage is used by permission of the Owatonna Orphanage Museum.

"How It All Began

"A New Welfare Policy\Minnesota Legislation—
1885

"The State Public School for Dependent and
Neglected Children was created by the legislature in 1885 as a state-of-the-art institution.
The act passed by the Minnesota Legislature
was almost an exact copy of the Michigan Law.
The State Public School in Coldwater, Michigan, was considered a model in every way.
Owatonna was chosen as the site for this new
school over eight other proposed sites due to its
easy access to railroads and its location near the
center of the most densely populated rural por-
tion of the state.

"Michigan's Philosophy

"Dependent children are not delinquent and
can be saved. Preventative measures such as
a pastoral environment and discipline could
render children deprived of a family acceptable
to a new family.

"Family-Like Life in Cottages

"Cottages will consist of approximately 25 children with a female matron as surrogate mother.
It is hoped the children will live in the cottage less than a year while eating in a common

dining room and working, playing, and praying together.

"Being Placed Out

"If possible, the dependent children 'after their basic training,' will be 'placed-out,' (adopted, fostered or indentured) preferably in rural homes. State agents will be responsible for selecting 'suitable homes' for the children, and for annual inspection thereafter of such placements.

"Education

"The State Public School will be a State Primary School where the children, until they can be adopted or indentured, can be educated morally and mentally, and also taught habits of industry.

"Emphasis on Discipline and Useful Labor

"Order, usefulness, and discipline will be stressed, as well as obedience and efficiency. Gentle and loving measures will be advocated, but the value of drill, discipline, and labor can never be underestimated.

"It is believed labor, no matter how dreary the task, or how paltry the remuneration, is good for the children. Each child, no matter the age, should be a part of some 'worth-while, demanding activity' each day.

"Michigan's Policies

"Adopted in Minnesota once admitted, children would become part of the following institutional system:

- Family-like life in cottages
- Placing-out programs
- Emphasis on discipline and useful labor
- Education

"A Self-Sustaining Institution

"At the height of its existence, the school housed 500 children in sixteen cottages. Other buildings included a nursery, hospital, school, gymnasium, laundry, and superintendent and employee residences. The school had its own power plant, greenhouse, icehouse, cemetery, and complete farm operation with cows, horses, swine, and chickens, making it virtually self-sufficient.

"The Main Building served as the nerve center of the school. Built in 1886 at a cost of $50,000, it housed the superintendent's office, staff offices, reception room, library, chapel, children and employees' dining rooms, industrial departments, and small boys' living quarters. The upper floors contained living quarters for employees.

"Originally housed on 160 acres, the grounds grew to 329 acres by 1937 with 42 acres for campus and 287 acres for farm cultivation.

"Orphanage Phased Out

"1945–1970

"Social changes caused the orphanage to be phased out by 1945. For the next twenty-five years, the school provided both academic and vocational programs for the educable mentally disabled.

"City of Owatonna Purchases Property

"After standing empty for four years, the city of Owatonna purchased the property in 1974 to house its city administrative offices and other related city facilities."

Courtship and the Start of Married Life 1940–1955

Helen Age 17 to 33

Meeting My Future Husband

When I was seventeen I met a young man who was twenty-three and from Romania. His Romanian name was Vasalie Choban but they called him Mitchell or Mike. He was born in the United States but when he was about nine his family moved back to Romania, and he remained there until he was twenty. He spoke very broken English. His friend went with my girlfriend and we double dated. On our dates we did things like going to movies or roller skating. After about six months he asked me to marry him. Come to think about it, I think he *told me* we were going to marry. He was a very demanding and controlling person. I remember one time I was smoking a cigarette and he got very angry and pulled it from my mouth and told me to never do that again. At the time this didn't bother me, as this had been what I was used to in my life. It was just another example of someone telling me what to do. Another time, after we were engaged, I got mad at him and threw my engagement ring out onto the lawn. He was furious and spent the rest of the night on his hands and knees searching through the grass for it. I don't know how much it cost, he got it at a pawn shop, but he was determined to find it and put it back on my finger.

The family I was working for and living with had a long talk with Mike and he told them many lies. My social worker met with Mike and Mrs. Hertz and based on those conversations the social worker thought he was a nice person. He told all of us the same lies. Here are a few excerpts from the social worker's home visits between August 29 and October 15, 1940.

> "Helen phoned the visitor [social worker] and reported that she had something she wanted to talk over. When visitor called she told her she had met a young man by the name of Mitchell Choban at a roller skating party. They were very fond of each other and were planning to be married in January. Mitchell Choban had wanted to get married before that, but Helen decided that she would be happier if she could get a few of the household furnishings together before their marriage, and she also felt that it was part of her responsibility to have a hope chest. Therefore, she had decided to discontinue

high school and secure a position where she could get more money and she would thus be able to get the things she wished. She apparently had thought the situation through carefully. Mitchell left the decision to her as to whether or not she wished to finish high school first.

"During the interview, Mrs. Hertz was present and she spoke of many things she had discussed with Helen about marriage. Before the decision was made, she had tried to get Helen to finish high school first. It was upon Mrs. Hertz's suggestion that Helen informed the visitor about her plans.

"Mitchell had been coming to the house regularly and Helen had met all of the relatives [I had only met one aunt of his] and had been at his home at 331 North Concord Street. [We had driven by the tavern and pool hall his father owned.] Mitchell's father is a contractor [not true, he owned a pool hall and bar] in South St. Paul and during the spring and summer, Mitchell works for his father and the balance of the year he is employed at the Swift [Meat] Packing Plant.

"Mitchell's mother is living in Europe. Mr. Choban [Mike's father] and his wife were married in the United States and returned to the old country [Romania]. As Helen understands it, Mrs. Choban was not interested in returning to the United States when Mr. Choban came back and the result was that Mr. Choban and Mitchell returned, leaving Mrs. Choban and some of the other children in Europe. Mitchell's uncle, a Mr. Choban, is one of the head men at the Drovers Bank, in South St. Paul, and he has another uncle who is working for Swift's. In Mrs. Hertz's opinion, Mitchell is a fine boy and all that she has been able to find out about his relatives has been creditable.

"Mitchell seemed to be certain that Helen could get a position at Swift's [Swift was a large meat packing plant] during the fall and they would then be married in January.

"When Helen presented her plans to the visitor she apparently had them all worked out so that it was not possible to discourage her or try to convince her that she should finish high school.

"On October third, visitor [social worker] noticed that a marriage license had been issued to Mitchell Choban and Helen Hoover. [There was a copy of the newspaper clipping announcing the marriage license in my file.]

"When Helen was interviewed, visitor talked over the matter of religion and marriage and pointed out the difference in their nationality and religious faith, but these were all things which Helen had already given considerable thought to.

"Mrs. Hertz reported that she had seen Helen since her marriage and that she seemed to be happy. They were temporarily living in light housekeeping rooms until they could secure an apartment. Helen had informed the visitor that Mitchell had purchased the furniture several months prior to their marriage and that he owned a house in South St. Paul. From the description it seemed to be a large old building and one which Mitchell had gotten as an interest in an estate, and he was buying it from the heirs."

Mike told me he owned a home, and his father was a contractor and had money. The truth was his father owned a tavern with pool tables in South St. Paul, Minnesota, about ten miles from St. Paul and the two of them lived in the same building. His father lived downstairs and Mike had one room upstairs. They rented out the other three rooms.

ENGAGEMENT AND THE
BEGINNING OF MARRIED LIFE

When my mother heard of my engagement she had me come up to Hurley, Wisconsin, about two hundred and fifty miles from St. Paul, and she gave a little wedding shower for me in late summer. She tried her best to talk me out of getting married. She had never met Mike but she decided she did not like him. He was a foreigner and did not speak English well. Mother thought I was too young to get married and wanted me to continue living with her. Also, Mike was calling almost every day to say he wanted to come to Hurley and bring me home. She said he was being controlling. I should have listened to her, but I didn't think she was much of a judge of men. She was on her second husband and they were living above a tavern. I think it is ironic that Mike and his father were living above a tavern just as my mother was. After a week with my mother I knew that wasn't where I wanted to be and went back to St. Paul. My trip to see mother made me very upset. Mike and I had planned to get married in January. I suppose it was the combination of rebelling against her and having nowhere to go, so I told Mike I wanted to get married right away.

Helen, Age 18

I never met my future father-in-law, Vasalie [also called Nick], before we got married. It didn't take me long to find out why. In no way were any of the Romanians going to welcome an American into the family. In their culture, if you were a Romanian you only married another Romanian. The only relative of Mike's that I knew was his aunt. She was a rebellious person and welcomed the chance to do something that would upset the family, so she encouraged me to go ahead with the wedding. I was married on October 7, 1930, in the Romanian Orthodox Church in St. Paul on my eighteenth birthday, not a word of English was spoken, and once again I did what I was told. His aunt and uncle stood up for us. We went on our honeymoon up in northern Minnesota and then I found out that he really did own me body and soul. We stayed at a little resort and went fishing. I didn't have a dime of my own and I had to come to him for everything. My life was not changing, just my keeper.

Mike did not want to come home, so we kept extending our honeymoon a few extra days. He was afraid to face his father, and I was terrified of how his father would treat me. We moved into the two rooms over the tavern. Even when I ate at the same table as his father, he spoke not a word to me. Mike worked in the tavern and shot pool for money.

I felt the power of Mike's fists shortly after we married. I was sitting on the arm of a chair showing his friend our wedding pictures. Mike came down the stairs and called me into the kitchen and knocked me over the kitchen table and said I was trying to make out with his friend. I was not surprised at being hit. I thought I had done something wrong and was being punished for it. I thought this was the way a husband treated his wife. That was to be the beginning of many beatings and this would take me deeper into the tunnel of dark.

Mike was a very jealous and controlling man. He couldn't let go of the old country ideas about how men treated women.

These ideas were that women had children, did as they were told, and were to be a servant to their husband. This wasn't too different from what my life had always been, so I didn't really try to change anything. There was one Romanian part of him that he did want to change and that was he wanted to lose his accent. I spent many hours with the dictionary and taught him to speak perfect English. By the time we were done he could speak with no accent at all. Permanent jobs were very hard to find and so Mike made some extra money going door to door selling Fuller Brush products.

Life beyond the tunnel came when an old man offered us a house if he could live with us. We jumped at the chance. We thought the rent we paid him would be applied as a down payment on the house when he decided to sell.

We needed money so I went looking for a job. I would go down to Swift Meat Packing Plant in South St. Paul every day trying to get hired. I would wait in line with the other people and hope that I was one of the few people that would be hired for the day. Finally I got a job and for the first time I had to do something other than housework. I went to work in the pork trim area. I would stand for eight hours a day on a cement floor in a room about forty degrees and trim the fat off half a pig carcass. I imagine these weighed at least fifty pounds, and after we trimmed them we had to move them to the next processing point. This was very hard work and especially difficult for women because it required so much strength. The rough language I heard was all new to me, and the women took joy in embarrassing me. After two months, I passed out on the floor and when I went to the doctor's office,

I found out I was pregnant. I told the doctor I could not be pregnant. I didn't even know how you got pregnant. Things like this were not talked about in the orphanage. Doctor Thorson told me I was the most uninformed child he had ever seen. I was surprised and not too happy because I was immature and very afraid of the future. I was just learning how to be a wife and now I would have to also be a mother. I continued to work right up to my time of delivery.

A SON MITCHELL (MITCH) IS BORN— JULY 19, 1941 • HELEN AGE 18

As I look back, I think that perhaps all the events going on in the world were an omen of how unsettled my oldest son's life would be. In the months before and after his birth the world was in turmoil. President Roosevelt declared an unlimited national emergency; the British sank the German battleship Bismarck; Germany invaded Russia; Roosevelt and Churchill met and drew up the Atlantic Charter; Col. Eisenhower led the first training maneuvers employing paratroopers; the Nazis ordered all Jews in Germany to wear Star of David.

Twenty-one hours of labor and finally I gave birth to the first boy in the Choban family. Now I was looked upon more favorably by my father-in-law. I named our son after my husband, Mitchell. I never thought my husband would change his name later in life. Mike had an uncle who was also named Mitchell Choban, and he was quite an important person in the Romanian community. It was confusing to have two Mitchells, so later my husband changed his name to Michael.

When my son was two months old, the man who owned the house we lived in (and thought we were buying from him) took himself a mail-order bride from Romania. She didn't take much time in letting us know we had to move out, so we went back to the one room at my father-in-law's store. We learned an important real estate lesson which was to get any agreements in writing.

After the baby was born I went back to work at Swift's while Mike took care of our son and continued to shoot pool for money. We saved up enough for a down payment on a house and we moved "up the hill." About this time I found out I was pregnant again. We bought a big house but rented out the three bedrooms upstairs and converted the dining room into the bedroom for our family. I did all the cleaning, changing linens, washing for our roomers. I remember one of our roomers was an elderly Hungarian woman who had a hot plate in the hall closet and did her cooking there. We had a continual aroma of garlic hanging over the whole house.

During this time my father-in-law became seriously ill, but he wouldn't go to the hospital unless I promised to run the tavern for him. He had a hernia and kept putting off the surgery until it got to be dangerously large and the doctors were afraid it would rupture. He said I was the only one he could trust. I knew nothing about running a tavern. The first time I drew a glass of beer, I almost drowned everyone at the bar. I would walk with my baby boy in tow every morning at 7:00 A.M. and open up the bar. I would clean spittoons, scrub floors, wash glasses, and do anything else that needed to be done. Mike was working at Swift's from 6:00 A.M. to 4:00 P.M. and needed to get some rest before he came to work at the tavern until midnight or later, depending on how busy it was. He did no cleaning up at home. That was a woman's work. I would have to walk one mile back home with my baby when he came to the tavern, then make meals for us, do the cleaning and washing. On weekends after my father-in-law got well, Mike decided to build a three-car concrete garage in our backyard. That way he could rent out two spaces. He was always looking for a way to get extra money. The two of us spent our Sundays building the garage. My hands got so cut up working with the bricks, but I still did as I was told. There were some fun times when we would go out for dinner or go fishing. Mike loved to fish.

A DAUGHTER ELIZABETH (BETTE) IS BORN— JULY 12, 1942 • HELEN AGE 19

I was married less then two years and had a one-year-old son and a beautiful new daughter. Bette was an easy birth, but the doctor advised me not to have any more children. After seeing many bruises on me he realized my life wasn't easy. Our living quarters were very small and our bedroom was also the nursery. I didn't like my first name, so when I named our daughter I gave her my middle name, Elizabeth. She didn't like that name, so when she got older she used the name Bette. She was a beautiful girl with curly hair and a real joy to me.

A Visit to See My Brother

I can remember this event so clearly. My brother Jack joined the air force and went to Walla Walla, Washington. He was the one brother who had not gone to the orphanage but was raised by my mother's parents in South Dakota. He and my mother stayed in contact with each other, and he had written me a few times so he knew I had gotten married and where I lived. He called me and said he was traveling through St. Paul on his way to England. I mentioned this to my neighbor, and she offered to take care of my children so I could go to the train depot. I was excited, but at the same time scared to be doing something without permission. I had not seen my brother since he was about four years old, but we knew each other right away. It was wonderful to see someone from my family.

I made sure I got home before Mike did, but I made the mistake of not removing all of my lipstick and as soon as he saw my pink lips he knew I had been someplace. I was standing by the stove and as I turned he swung and hit me flush on my mouth and knocked me out. He knocked out for my four front teeth, cracked my jawbone on the right side, and bruised my cheekbones. I was a real mess. When I came to, he was telling me how this beating was my fault. He said I should know better than to do things without permission. I remember soon after this we went to a party at his aunt's, and I told her I hit my face on the dashboard of the car. She said she had a pretty good idea what really happened, and she knew what the men in the family were like. After that, it was years before he would allow me to go uptown by myself. The only bright light in my tunnel was my two wonderful children.

I lived in fear of the beatings and getting pregnant. The doctor told me not to have any more children for a few years. Another incident I remember was when I had been talking with one of the roomers. I came downstairs and Mike was furious about something I had, or had not, done and came up and pushed me down the whole flight of steps and then kicked me until I passed out. The next day when I had to go to the doctor, the doctor called a lawyer, Harold Le Vander, and said something had to be done or my husband would kill me.

About this time Mike decided he didn't like working at Swift. He wanted his own business. He bought three buildings. One was a drugstore, one a grocery store, and the third was a small adjoining building that he made into a three-room apartment. He rented out the apartment and the drugstore and decided we should run the grocery store. He didn't have a very good personality when it came to dealing with people. It is not very good customer service if the owner is always right and the customer is always wrong. Mike would work in the store all day, and I would go back and forth between watching the children in our apartment and helping him in the store. We had a butcher who ran the meat department. If Mike heard me laugh with him, he would come in the back of the store and give me a dirty look. He was so jealous. When we were alone he would slap me around and was always telling me what I was doing was wrong. We were open seven days a week so there was little time to play with my children.

REFLECTION AND INFORMATION

What does an abused woman with two small children and few skills do in 1940? Where do I go? What do I do? Domestic violence was not a topic anyone was talking about. It's not like today when you see it written about in newspapers and magazines. If there were organizations that could help me, I did not know about them. I was so afraid someone would call me a bad mother and take away my babies. After Mike would beat me, he would always say how sorry he was and then would want to have sex. All this time he would tell me how lucky I was that he married me because I was just someone nobody else wanted. After I heard this for so long, I believed what he was saying was true. I was so alone and unwanted. It is really dark in the tunnel. I see no way out and feel trapped. Were it not for my kids, I might give up.

CHILDHOOD ILLNESS—1944 • HELEN AGE 22

In early 1944 Mitch got rheumatic fever. At that time, children with this disease were kept in bed and not allowed to walk or do anything. I got teenage girls in the neighborhood to play with him so I could do the housework. Mitch recovered from this, but then on Christmas Eve he again became very ill. Not knowing what was wrong, the doctor put him in the hospital and operated on him for appendicitis. His appendix was twice the size of an adult's and black, and he was full of cysts. The doctor did as much as he could, sewed him up, and told us to pray. They told us there was a slim chance that he would live. We called Rochester Medical Clinic in Rochester, Minnesota, to see if the doctor would come up, but they said no and gave us very little hope. I stayed at the hospital and slept in one of the old wooden wheelchairs with the back that tilted. He was in the hospital for three weeks and when we came home, the doctor advised us to get a house where the children could be outside and get fresh air. The place we were living had no windows. Mike's answer to that was "nobody tells me what do." That summer of 1945 the polio epidemic broke out and Mitch was still not well, so Mike finally agreed to send both children and me to Frederic, Wisconsin, to the stay on a farm with my father's elderly aunt and uncle.

THE ACCIDENT—1946 • HELEN, AGE 24

While at the farm in Frederic, Mitch, Bette, and I were riding on a wagon out to pick up hay. We had done this a number of times. The horses started to run away. My two children fell under the iron wheels of the hay rack. My young cousin was driving the horses and he fell down on the tongue and almost got trampled to death. We got the children back to the farmhouse and called the doctor and the ambulance, which in those days also served as a hearse. My aunt and uncle had gone to a funeral in town and heard what had happened on the farm. My aunt was very upset and had a heart attack. Fortunately, she recovered.

When we got into the ambulance/hearse, the doctor told me to start praying as both of my babies were dying. Up to this time I didn't have much of a relationship with God. I didn't really think he even knew I existed, and I sure didn't think he loved me. But pray I did and real hard.

The doctor's examination showed that Mitch had a broken collar bone and his broken ribs had made a hole in one of his lungs, and there was no way to set any of the bones. Bette had almost all the bones in her body broken from the collarbone to her pelvic bone. She was bleeding internally, and there was little chance she would survive. I broke my ankle, but that hardly seemed to matter. I slept on a mattress on the floor in their hospital room. I called my mother in Portland, Oregon, and my father in Spokane, Washington, and they both came to Frederic. It was the first time they met in about fourteen years. I was surprised at how congenial they were with each other. The children were in the hospital about two months and my parents stayed for a couple weeks until the children were out of danger. When they were finally well enough to leave the hospital, we went back to Frederic so they could continue to recover. God apparently had other plans for these two kids. I felt very bad about my sick children, but even under these circumstances I was happy because I was free and away from Mike, and I really enjoyed the life on the farm.

Trip to My Mother's

While we were recuperating in Frederic, Wisconsin, Mike sold the businesses and all our furniture. He said he wanted the money. I never knew what he wanted it for. He said I should take the kids and go to Portland, Oregon, to visit my mother. By this time I found out Mike had several girlfriends in his life and wanted the children and me to make the trip without him so he could spend time with his girlfriends.

The trip to Portland on the train was my first time out on my own, and I was petrified but thrilled to be with my children all by myself. We had such a great time on the trip out, although sleeping three in the train bunks was a bit crowded. I was excited about staying with my mother, but scared as I had never met my stepfather, Frank, and didn't know what the reception will be like. Our train was very late in getting into Portland, and there was no one to meet us. Now I was really scared and thinking, "What if she changed her mind and does not want me here?" I took a cab out to her house. When we pulled up the yard was filled with beautiful daffodils. They are still one of my favorite flowers.

My mother lived in a housing project with very cramped quarters. It was exciting at first, but after a few weeks of being with a woman I hardly knew, who was giving orders not only to me but also to my children, this life with her was not sitting too well with me. She continually berated Mike and told me to leave him. This was not what I wanted to hear. I figured when you got married, you stayed married. I knew what divorce did to a family. I had lived it with the multiple marriages and divorces of my parents.

Mike bought a Cadillac and came out to get us. Our trip home would only reinforce his opinion that my family was no good. We were taking my grandfather to my aunt's home in Minneapolis. Our first stop was in Kellogg, Idaho. My three aunts lived there with their husbands. One family owned a tavern, and I was to learn they were all heavy drinkers. They decided to take Mike out for a night on the town, which lasted for two days. This was not to my liking. These people were like strangers and not the loving relatives I was hoping to find.

The next stop was at the state prison in Montana so grandpa could see his son who was in prison for holding up a filling station. This last stop really cemented all Mike's thoughts of my family. I heard all the way home how rotten my family was and no wonder I turned out like I did. I was sorry I had ever gone to visit them. After wanting a family all those years, it was really a disappointment. It was a miserable trip home.

REFLECTION AND INFORMATION

It seems that much of my life was spent with sick children and dealing with my own illnesses. I was only twenty-four years old and had no experience dealing with the challenges that were ahead of me. I think now that these early tests of my strength as a mother and as a woman helped me get the courage to deal with the adversity in my life. Instead of being weakened by these experiences I became strong.

With a few exceptions, like my sisters-in-law, I was very much alone. Mike disapproved of all of my family, and I had limited contact with them. I'm going further into the tunnel. I can see no light in my life except for my children.

Running Away—1946 • Helen, Age 24

Mike had spent all our money on the new car and other women. We had no choice but move back to the two rooms upstairs in my father-in-law's tavern. The place was even worse than it was when we left it four years earlier. The furniture was two cribs, one broken day bed, and one mattress, on the floor, which I slept on. I can't possibly describe the horrible conditions under which we lived. Between the mice and the cockroaches, I lived in fear of my children's safety all the time.

Mike would not find a job, but I found one at a toy factory. He took care of the children, played pool, tended bar, and complained because I didn't make more money. My children spent a great deal of time with Mike at the tavern and could name every brand of whiskey and beer ever sold. This was their education from their father.

Every Friday night I would come home with my paycheck and hand it over to Mike. By now I was out among other people and knew I wasn't living a normal life. One Friday night, I decided, "He isn't going to get my paycheck." My little son, Mitch, grabbed my purse and his father grabbed him and threw him across the room. This really did it for me. It was one thing to abuse me, but he was not going to do the same thing to my children. I reached for the first thing I could get my hands on which was a glass soda pop bottle and hit him over the head. It just dazed him and he came after me. Little Mitch went screaming down the stairs to get his grandfather. Mike left the house and did not come home all night. In the morning I packed up as much as I could carry and took my two children and left.

I knew I had to do something or all of our lives were in danger. I remembered I had an Aunt Mildred in Minneapolis. She was my mother's sister, the only one who really amounted to anything, and I was to learn later she wanted to adopt me when we were taken away from our parents. My mother wouldn't approve that adoption because her sister was Catholic and my mother was Presbyterian. I called Aunt Mildred and told her my circumstances. She said my cousin would be right over to pick us up. My father-in-law saw us leave, but by this time I think he had seen enough of what my life was like and he did not try to stop us. My aunt was so wonderful. She and her husband already had six children but they fit the three of us into their home. I continued to work at a toy factory, and my aunt took care of my children.

I was in contact with a good lawyer, Harold LeVander, who later became a Minnesota governor. He lived in South St. Paul and knew my circumstances through my doctor. I wanted to leave the state to see my mother, but Mr. LeVander told me I couldn't go or Mike could charge me with kidnapping. I never spoke to Mike about this aunt so he had no idea where I might be. Mike called my mother in Portland, and all our friends but could not find me. Mr. LeVander was in contact with Mike and told him he needed to send me money and get a decent job and a home before I would consider coming back. Mr. LeVander made Mike give him the money and then Mr. LeVander gave the money to me. I don't think I am exaggerating when I say that Harold LeVander saved my life. If it were not for him I would have made some very bad decisions. He was about the only person who had shown any empathy for me. He was also at some risk himself. The Choban name was quite influential in South St. Paul, but Mr. LeVander did not seem to care about that.

Mike was having a hard time accepting the fact that he did not have control of me and the children. At last my husband realized he could lose everything. His wife, children, and the respect of the Romanian community would all be gone. He was a very proud man, and this was not what he wanted.

Mike must have listened to Mr. LeVander because he took a job with a real estate company, and he found a small two-bedroom home that was completely furnished and right across the street from the school. He called the lawyer and asked him to contact me and see if we could get back together. The situation sounded even better when the lawyer told me about the deal he had made with Mike whereby, if he ever beat me up again, he would go to jail. After five long months of working, helping my aunt, and keeping my two children happy, everything was taking a toll on me physically and mentally. With these pieces in place, I went back to Mike. I became active in PTA and made friends with other mothers and felt as if I had a little life of my own. Things were good. Mike decided to open his own real estate business in the basement of our home. He still controlled the money situation completely, but this didn't bother me as long as I had some freedom with my children. I could see some light in the tunnel.

REFLECTION ON HAROLD LEVANDER

Little did I know in 1944 when I was referred to a young lawyer, thirty-four, in South St. Paul, that he would one day become the governor of Minnesota. I am so thankful to my doctor who had the good sense to refer me to such a good lawyer. I think the world is a better place because of leaders like Mr. LeVander. He certainly made my world better.

ROBERT (BOB, MY SECOND SON) IS BORN— JULY 23, 1948 • HELEN, AGE 26

The years passed by and Mitch was seven and Bette was six. I became pregnant with our third child. I was happy because the other two were going to school, and it was a little lonely at home. On July 23, 1948, Robert was born.

Bob was born perfectly normal at birth but while up north on a fishing vacation things changed dramatically. I remember we were up at the lake. Bob was about two and just starting to learn how to run. He was so cute trying to help out by carrying in fire wood. I noticed he had a mosquito bite. The result of this bite was that he was infected with spinal meningitis. It took the doctors five months to identify the cause of his illness. During this time he would run a high fever, between 103 and 105 degrees, for weeks at a time. I would have to give him alcohol baths to keep him from convulsions. He was in the hospital many times for a variety of tests, but no one seemed to know what the problem was. The last specialist had him in Children's Hospital in Minneapolis, where his fever hit 107, and he hemorrhaged in the brain. He could no longer walk, feed himself, or sit up by himself. He became a helpless baby again. He was diagnosed as having cerebral palsy. These diseases were to have a big impact on Bob and me.

The next six years would be devoted to constant therapy with Bob. When the doctor first told me my son had cerebral palsy, I was devastated. Telling Mike was my greatest fear, because I knew he would blame me. My fears came true when he ranted and raved and said nobody was to see Bob until I made him "human." To have a son who was anything but perfect was a disgrace. When we had company, Mike wanted me to hide Bob in the closet.

Mike was making money with his real estate business. He definitely had his own ideas of what that money would be spent on, and gave me an allowance to take care of the children, and the house. He shared very little of our financial situation with me. He wanted Bob to be normal so I got the money to get rehabilitation and therapy for Bob. Mike never went to the rehabilitation center or to a doctor's visit with me. My friends would come over and help with the creep-crawl exercises that Bob had to do to help him learn coordination and gain strength. This exercise is just like its description. We would move Bob's arms and legs like he was crawling. His muscles were so weak, and we had to strengthen them as well as teach him coordination and retrain his brain to do all the things he had been able to do before he got sick. We would have to do these exercises for hours on end. All this time I would take him to the rehab center five times a week. Bob did not have to wear braces but he did need a brace to help him sit in a chair. It was so heartbreaking to see him struggle to hold his head up. These times were hard on the older children, as all my time was given to their younger brother.

A Daughter Barbara (Barb) is Born— January 23, 1951 • Helen, Age 28

Why another child? I didn't want to raise Bob without someone to keep him company. His other brother and sister were quite a bit older and had their own friends. It would be good for Bob to have someone to play with, even though it was hard for him.

When he was two and a half, I gave birth to another girl. Bob and Barb grew up very close. Barb was a beautiful child with big blue eyes and curly hair. My children were my life. They were the only light in my tunnel and for a short while I felt as if I was at least holding my life together.

At this time we moved into a new home, partly finished. What an ordeal. We ate in the basement with the plaster falling through the floorboards and into our plates. We heated the upstairs bedrooms with a kerosene heater that backed up and put a layer of soot all over the walls, beds, and floors.

Mike now had his own real estate and construction company. Other people thought we were rich, and maybe we were, but it didn't mean much to the children and me as we lived on a very tight budget. Mike did agree to spend some extra money, and we hired my girlfriend's mother to come and live with us so I had time to take care of Bob and Barb. This was really nice, as it also gave me more time to spend with the older children. Those two older ones were really very special. They didn't complain or seem to resent the time I had to spend with Bob. They would never get used to having spilled milk at every meal, as we tried to teach Bob to hold a glass. The four of them still laugh over what life at the dinner table with Bob was like.

I started to get active in the United Cerebral Palsy Association. I worked on a telethon that Bob appeared in when he was four years old, and when asked what they taught him at the rehab center, he replied "not to spit." This was his biggest accomplishment up to this time. He thought that not to always drool and have to wear a bib was great.

During all this time Mike still didn't want his business associates to see Bob; only our closest friends or relatives saw him.

MORE CHILDHOOD ILLNESS— 1952 • HELEN, AGE 30

You would think by now God had given me and my children enough tests. This was not the case. When Bob was four, he got rheumatic fever and was hospitalized, and, at almost the same time, Barbara, who was one and a half, woke up one night crying, and the whole side of her face was distorted. The doctor informed me she had Bell's Palsy. This is a condition that causes facial muscles to weaken or become paralyzed. My life seemed to be falling apart.

When the doctor told me what was happening with the children, I screamed and asked "Why me? How do I tell Mike?" When I told Mike, he responded as expected with hollering about how it was my fault. I was evil, no good, no wonder my parents gave me away and all the words I had heard before.

For the next two months Bob and Barb were at Children's Hospital in St. Paul in beds side by side. I would go up every day to see them. Barb was the pet of the nurses and the day her face went back to normal was a great celebration for everyone. All this time the older children were on their own growing up much too fast. Bette had to assume a great deal of responsibility for running our home.

GETTING BOB INTO A SCHOOL— 1954 • HELEN, AGE 32

When Bob was old enough to start school, I was told he would have to go to a special school. The problem was we had to live in the city of St. Paul or he could not attend. I couldn't see moving and disrupting our two older children. I began my fight for mandatory education for all children. I spoke to the education committee at the state capitol and tried to explain to them that these children were just like they were—they had red blood, cried real tears, and had to be let out of their closets and given the chance to go to school and live a normal life.

Next, I went to the school board in South St. Paul. They said if the principal of the local school was willing to give Bob a chance, then he could go to school. Bob had a sharp mind but the body was weak. He had a hard time walking and running and still drooled when he was concentrating on something real hard. He had typical cerebral palsy body actions.

The teachers from the South St. Paul school really took Bob under their wings and gave him special attention. This seemed great at the time, but in the long run he learned bad habits. He really got by with a lot until about sixth grade. At that time he had a new teacher, Mr. Saari, who knew nothing about Bob except he could see that Bob wasn't applying himself to his school work. We hired Mr. Saari to come to the house twice a week to tutor Bob and improve his study habits.

DEPRESSION, SHOCK, AND INSULIN TREATMENTS—1955 • HELEN, AGE 33

You can go through the daily routine of life even when you are depressed. The feelings of despair and hopelessness came on gradually. When I look back now, I realize that I was already depressed five years earlier, before Barb was born, and I was exhausted from dealing with Bob and his illness and therapy. I was very unhappy because I wanted to do so much for my family and be a good mother and things were not working out that way. I thought everything that happened was my fault because that is what I was told. It was more than I could handle with no help. I weighed only eighty-eight pounds. I was so exhausted and weak, and the doctors thought I had polio. The tunnel was so deep and dark now that I thought suicide was the only way out. I started to see a psychiatrist, Dr. Flom.

When I was thirty-three the psychiatrist told me I had to go to the hospital for tests. Of course, it did not occur to me to question the doctor, or Mike, about it. I got out of the elevator on the eighth floor of the hospital and saw the gate of the psychiatric floor. I already felt that I had been locked up in the orphanage; the thought of being institutionalized again terrified me. I panicked and screamed, "Why are you doing this to me? Don't lock me up again."

By then my weight had dropped to seventy-five pounds, and I was told I had a nervous breakdown. I had twelve electric shock treatments and thirty insulin shock treatments. The electric shock treatments occurred about once a week. I always knew when they were going to give me a treatment. The doctor would come in with his black bag and six nurses would follow him in. They would attach the electric wires to my head and the doctor would say, "Ok, Helen, here we go." The nurses would hold me down because I would go into convulsions. During shock treatment they send an electric current to your brain and these result in grand mal or major epileptic seizures. The brain waves go flat, just like in brain death. I would be unconscious for the rest of the day. After I got the first shock treatment, my hair turned white overnight. I sure wasn't prepared for that to happen.

After the series of twelve electric shock treatments, they started the insulin shock treatments. I think I got those almost every night. They give you a shot of insulin and this makes your blood sugar level drop low enough to cause a coma and sometimes a convulsion. I would be in and out of reality all night. I would talk to myself, and they would record it. I would say things like, "I have to be a better wife. I know I can do this." And then the opposite, "Why am I here? I am a good wife." In the morning I would get a big glass of orange juice with dextrose in it and that would bring me out of it. It was terrible. My mind would struggle all night. I remember begging for water.

The doctors thought that my breakdown and depression was caused by my fear of my husband and always trying to do right by everyone. My childhood played a big part in all of this also. I had been abandoned so many times. I didn't cry when the doctor talked about my beatings, but when they asked me about my childhood I would always cry. They thought the way to get me well was to take away my memories. It worked. I didn't want to go home. I had been there for six months. I had fun in the hospital. We played games, played musical instruments, and danced. I felt free and didn't have any responsibility, and I loved it. I didn't want it to end.

Mitch was fourteen and going to be confirmed, and I was given a one-day release from the hospital so I could go to church. I went to church and had to sit in the front of the church because I still could not stand to be around people. I felt safer in the front because it seemed more like I was by myself. Something happened to scare me, and I started screaming and crying in the church, and Mike had to take me back to the hospital.

When I did finally come home, I didn't recognize my house, but I did know my children. My childhood memories were gone. This is one of the very darkest times in my tunnel. It was also very difficult for my children. Mike would not hire anyone to help me, so the burden fell on my daughter Bette, only thirteen.

A few years passed since my first breakdown and I was a little better, but every day was a struggle. I still had no confidence in myself, felt like I was all alone, and thought that God had forsaken me. It was 1960 and I was getting ready for a bowling banquet, which Mike disapproved of. I remember leaving for the banquet, and the next thing I knew I was in a strait jacket in Mounds Park Hospital. I had tried to commit suicide. The first thing I said was, "Did I hurt my children?" The doctor said no and added, "You have a brilliant mind, and you are not using it right. Why do you do these things?" I said, "Do what things?" I could not remember anything. All I ever wanted to be was a good mother, and if I was a good mother I would automatically be a good wife. That was my thought process.

I never did find out what happened. I went back into the hospital for about two months and had electric shock therapy and insulin shock treatments again, and this time I was also given truth serum. When I went home my memory was gone again. I did not remember my friends, but did remember my children. I was still in my tunnel where it was dark, and I was confused. I remember thinking that these feelings of despair would never end and that this is what the rest of my life would be like.

As if that was not enough, when I was forty years old, I started having epileptic seizures. This was devastating thing for me. My father and brothers Jack and Dick and Jack's daughter and grandson were also epileptic. Years before I saw my father have a seizure. He was a chef at a hotel, and he had us over for Thanksgiving dinner. We sat down to eat and he looked at me. I said, "Dad what's the matter?" He said, "Why are you here? Go away. I don't know who you are, and I don't want you in my room." Jack said, "He is going into a seizure," so when I had my seizure I knew what it was. At first my seizures were a couple of times a week, but eventually I got to the point where medication controlled them pretty well. I have continued on medication and now only occasionally have seizures. Our family was part of a University of Minnesota study to find out why it ran in families.

REFLECTION AND INFORMATION
ON MY TREATMENTS

To this day electric shock and insulin shock treatments are controversial. The way the treatments are given has improved since I had them, and the medical profession continues to say they are safe, but it seems that for every "expert" testimony of the procedure's safety there are other "experts" and many patients who have received the treatment that say it did long-term damage, including permanent memory loss.

When I finally saw that movie *Snake Pit*, which came out in 1948 with Olivia de Havilland, I remember thinking that this was me. I could see myself in that situation. I have been thinking back about the orphanage and when I went to Dr. Flom, my psychiatrist, for the therapy sessions and shock treatments. It really wasn't fair for him to take my memory away. I do believe that it was the best treatment they knew at the time for severe depression. It has only recently become apparent to me how much it did affect my memory. I now know that I lost four years completely. The memories of when I was about four to eight years old are gone. I remember a few things, like eating raw potatoes in the basement, but I don't remember going to school, having any playmates, details of living with my parents and brothers, or being taken to the Presbyterian orphanage. I will never know what I don't remember, but perhaps it is just as well.

Bringing Natalia
from Romania
1958

Helen Age 40

One of the most interesting times in my marriage was when we were trying to get Mike's family out of Romania. Romania, also called Rumania, was under Communist and Russian control. To say that life in Romania was difficult is an understatement. It is primarily an agricultural country and the heavy hand of the Communists and Russians controlled the people, their lives, and their property. Romania remains today one of the least developed of the European countries.

MIKE'S FAMILY

Mike had three brothers, George, John, Nick; one sister, Paulina; and his mother, Natalia, living in Romania. His father,

Vasalie or Nick, lived here in the United States. All the children, except John, were conceived and born in the United States and became American citizens. Natalia then moved back to Romania with the children. The children were schooled in Romania, but had to return to the United States by the time they were twenty-one. I think this was so they could maintain their United States citizenship. Vasalie, my father-in-law, remained in the United States and worked and sent money to Romania for the family. Mike felt this was a normal way of living.

My father-in-law felt it was his job to get his family out of Romania and legally into the United States. This meant providing passage from Romania, clothing, housing, and jobs for them. While Vasalie might have felt responsible, it fell to Mike, being the oldest and best established, to actually get everything set up for his family. Mike came first in 1936 and by 1950 the last brother, John, arrived here. Since John was not a citizen, he faced additional problems getting here. By 1950, the Communist Party control was very strict on letting people out. The story I heard was that John had connections with the Romanian underground, and eventually he used these connections to escaped to Germany and then to the United States. This left Mike's sister, who was married and had a family, and his mother in Romania. Eventually these brothers got married, and had children. I began to feel as if I finally had a family. Having sisters–in-law was fun, and we had good times together, but couldn't get too close. We always got together at holidays, church dinners, and picnics.

My mother-in-law couldn't write or speak English. When she wrote Mike, I'd look at the letters and when I would see my name I'd ask what she had written about me. Sometimes he would tell me, but most of the time he would not.

Natalia wanted to leave but the Romanian government would not let her out of the country. We did not realize how bad it was until word got to us from a friend of ours who had relatives over there. He confirmed our worst fears of how bad things were. There was not enough food and the living conditions were very poor. We would send her mail, medicine, and other packages, but the Communists confiscated all of this. We sent medicine for Mike's niece who we were told had cancer. She never got it. We would send Natalia airplane tickets, but she was never allowed to use them. Finally, the Communists took the Choban family's small farm and put Natalia in a detention camp. She would remain there for five years.

SENATOR HUBERT H. HUMPHREY AND THE RED CROSS

After trying unsuccessfully for eleven years to get her over here, I turned to our United States senator, Hubert H. Humphrey, for help. There were several letters I have from Senator Humphrey, the Red Cross, and the American Consulate. I include them to help you understand what we were facing. Here is the letter I received from Senator Humphrey dated October 16, 1947. However, I think the date is an error and should be 1957.

"Dear Mrs. Choban:

"Thank you for your letter regarding your mother-in-law's visa. I shall certainly be glad to try to speed up the processing of her application. It seems to me that eight years is a distressingly long wait.

"I have asked our Ambassador in Bucharest to look into the matter for me and send me a report. As soon as I have any news, I will let you know.

Best wishes.

Sincerely yours,

Hubert H. Humphrey"

On October 17, 1957, Senator Humphrey received a letter from Graham D. Renner, American Vice Consul, that said Natalia's visa had expired and needed to be revalidated, but they were working on it.

On November 7, 1957, the American Consulate in Bucharest Romania sent Senator Humphrey this letter.

"Dear Senator Humphrey:

"This will acknowledge receipt of your letter of October 30, 1957, concerning Mrs. Nick Choban, a prospective immigrant.

"It is almost eleven years now since Mrs. Choban's case first came to our attention. Like all people who have tried to get out of Rumania, she has had a discouraging time. As the wife of a naturalized American citizen she had a non-quota immigrant status and will be able to proceed to the United States as soon as the Rumanians agree to give her a passport and an exit permit. When they will be willing to do so is impossible to judge, but the only thing I can say is that the situation is more hopeful today than it has been for some time since in the past few weeks several persons in cases similar to that of Mrs. Choban have been granted the necessary papers to leave. I hesitate, however, to prophecy in any of these cases. I can only say that we have been and will continue to bring all possible pressures to bear upon the Rumanian Foreign Office to release her.

"When we receive any good news I will be glad to let you know immediately. As of possible assistance in expediting her case with the Rumanian authorities, I suggest that Mr. Choban might ask the American Red Cross to get in touch with the Rumanian Red Cross through the International Red Cross in Geneva and request them to intervene with the Rumanian authorities in his wife's behalf. The Rumanian Red Cross recently has shown some interest in being active in these cases. Also, as a last resort, there is the question of publicity. We have had some indication that the Rumanians cannot stand the full glare of publicity being put upon cases of divided families and will act if a real public hue and cry is put up.

"Assuring you of our continued cooperation in these and all other cases of this kind. I am

Sincerely yours,
Robert H. Thayer
Minister"

On January 15, 1958, the American National Red Cross in Washington D.C. wrote this letter to Senator Humphrey.

"My dear Senator Humphrey:

"This is in reply to your letter of January 7, 1958, concerning Mrs. Nick Choban, a prospective immigrant from Rumania. The American Red Cross has been working closely with the Rumanian Red Cross to facilitate the early reunion of dispersed families. I am glad to report that we have received excellent cooperation from the Rumanian Red Cross and in recent weeks several of the individuals in whose behalf we have asked their assistance have arrived in the United States.

"As you know, the issuance of an exit permit is a question for the Rumanian government authorities. However, when there has been a long delay in acting on an application, the Rumanian Red Cross may intervene with their government authorities basing their appeal on humanitarian grounds. If Mr. Choban wishes us to do so, we will be glad to present his wife's case to the Rumanian Red Cross with a request for their assistance in expediting her early departure from the country to be reunited with her family in the United States.

"If Mr. Choban decides to do this, it will be necessary to have accurate information concerning Mrs. Choban's full name, birth date, present address in Rumania, the date on which she applied for an exit states visa application. I suggest that Mr. Choban send this information directly to Miss Mary Lightle, International Relations Assistant, American Red Cross, Washington, D.C., who is the person at our national headquarters working on the reunion of families.

Sincerely,
Alfred M. Gruenther"

There is a hand written note on the bottom of the letter dated January 16, 1958, which says: *"Talked with Miss Lightle—they have now received all data from their chapter in Minnesota on this case. Will probably take three months mos. [months]."*

In November 1958, I received these letters, one from Senator Humphrey, and the other a letter which he received.

The following letter was enclosed and is from the American Legation [A diplomatic office or headquarters in a foreign country], Bucharest, Rumania, and dated October 27, 1958.

"Dear Senator Humphrey:

"The receipt is acknowledged of your letter of October 15, 1948, in which you renewed your interest in the immigrant visa case of Mrs. Natalia CIBAN. [sic]

"The legation is pleased to inform you that Mrs. Cioban [sic] has now received her travel documentation from the Rumanian authorities and that this office is therefore prepared to formally process her visa application. The approved Visa Petition filed on behalf of Mrs. Cioban [sic] had, however expired and was forwarded to the Immigration and Naturalization Service for revalidation. You may rest assured that as soon as the Petition is returned, final action will be taken on this case.

"Sincerely Yours,
Graham D. Renner
American Vice Consul"

This is the letter from Senator Humphrey and is dated November 4, 1958.

"Dear Mrs. Choban:

"We have just received the attached report from Bucharest about Mrs. Nick Choban's visa application.

"I am so glad to see that final action can soon be taken, and I trust that my wire to the St. Paul

Office of Immigration will speed revalidation of
the petition which your father-in-law filed for her.
They can take care of this without bothering you.

"Sincerely Yours,
Hubert H. Humphrey"

NATALIA ARRIVES IN THE UNITED STATES

It is now mid December 1958, and everything was planned
for her arrival. When we checked with Kennedy airport in
New York, we found out she wasn't on the scheduled flight.
For reasons unknown to us she was taken off in Prague,
Czechoslovakia. Through his Washington D.C. office, we
contacted Senator Humphrey again for help. Senator Humphrey was on a tour in Romania about this time, and I am
sure he used his influence again and got her passage on a
flight out of Czechoslovakia. Once again he came through
and she was on the way. I have always felt bad that he could
not have been here to see her arrival.

The family was gathered at the Wold Chamberlain Airport
in Minneapolis. In 1985, the terminal, upon completion of
a major expansion, was renamed the Charles A. Lindbergh
Terminal after the famous aviator, a Minnesota native. We
waited to welcome this little frail lady, dressed in her long
dress, apron, and babushka on her head. She wore a jacket
made of horse hair and carried all her worldly possessions in
a mesh bag. Meeting her family, some of whom she had not
seen in twenty years, was frightening for both her and her
family. There were lots of hugs, tears of joy, and kisses.

Here is the article and photo from the *Minneapolis Morning Tribune* on December 19, 1958.

Mr. and Mrs. Nick Choban

"Mrs. Ana Natalia Choban, 58, was reunited with her husband and four sons for the first time in nearly 27 years Thursday at Wold Chamberlain airport.

"The short, travel-weary woman, sobbing with joy and shivering in the icy Minnesota wind, stepped off a Northwest Airline's plane about 2:15 p.m. Immediately she was engulfed by her husband, Nick, 69, South St. Paul, her four sons, all of South St. Paul, her sister, Mrs. Paulina Stefan, St. Paul, and her sons' families.

"She had left San Nico Laul Mare, Romania, seven days before.

"Mrs. Choban, who spent five years in a Communist detention camp in Romania, had last seen her husband in 1932. She recognized only her youngest son, John, who left Romania and his mother in 1950.

"Her arrival in the Twin Cities yesterday climaxed years of struggle by her husband through war, political upheaval, and conflicting family ties to unite his family here.

"Choban, a Romanian emigrant, met his wife in Chicago in 1915 shortly after she came from Romania. They moved to South St. Paul after their marriage and prospered.

"In 1926 the family visited the old country— Choban, his wife, and their three sons, Michael, George, and Nick, Jr. After a year in Romania, a fourth son, John, was born.

"In 1930 the couple returned to the United States. In 1932 Mrs. Choban went back to join their children, but Choban had to remain in this country.

"Michael was the first son to return to the United States, coming in 1936. George followed in 1939. Nick Jr., came in 1947, and John in 1950.

"Mrs. Choban asked for permission to follow, but ownership of a small farm complicated matters.

"In 1952 the Communists confisticated her property. She was put in a detention camp, later lived with a daughter.

"She finally made it to the United States after action by the Red Cross and Sen. Humphrey (D. Minn.)

"The Chobans' daughter, Paulina, remains in
Romania. She is married and has a family."

The following months were both fun and work. Her trip to
the United States was quite a media event. A local television
station got interested in her story, and we went with them on
a shopping trip. When you add in camera crew, interpreter,
and the family all together it was a once-in-a life time experience. She wouldn't do anything or go any place without me.
She felt closer to me than anyone else. She hadn't worn very
feminine clothes for many years and wasn't receptive to anything I suggested. Trying on shoes that weren't a man's shoe
was one of the hardest tasks she had. But trying on shoes was
nothing next to getting her on an escalator. She absolutely
refused and kept trying to get off. I did finally get her to go
into an elevator. These were all new, strange, and frightening experiences for her.

The most fun Natalia had these first months was going to
the grocery store. Cookies, cookies, and more cookies, especially chocolate ones, were her favorite. She would automatically go to the cookie section and start loading up the cart.
She would become very agitated when I would say no. This
frail little lady of ninety pounds soon started the upward
climb to two hundred pounds, mostly by eating all the new
sweets and fatty foods that she wasn't used to.

All those years that her husband had been in the United
States, he kept sending money to her in Romania, so by
Romanian standards she lived quite well, at least until the
Communists took over, and she had a hard time getting used

to living in a four-room apartment with a man she hardly knew anymore. She didn't understand why she couldn't have a big house like Mike. She had envisioned the United States as a land of plenty and felt she wasn't getting her share of the wealth of this new country. She wanted a summer cabin like we had, and a place where she could have a garden. I tried to explain how hard we have all worked for what we had in our homes, but she wasn't buying any of that. She continually told me how selfish I was. Not her son, just me. After three years, she decided she wanted to go back to Romania for a visit. She still had her mother, a daughter, and grandchildren there. We went on another shopping trip, this time buying items for the relatives. We packed up boxes and boxes of things and shipped them to Romania. Natalia also wanted to take some personal items. I was the only one who had luggage, so she went with my new luggage. Our family had traveled but had used only cardboard boxes for years, so I really treasured my luggage.

After three weeks she came home from Romania, getting off the plane with her mesh bag in hand. My first question was, "Where's my luggage?" "I gave it to them [her relatives]; they liked it." When I complained, she told that me I was selfish.

Natalia ruled the family. She was feisty by nature and had been on her own in Romania for many years. She had learned how to be independent. My father-in–law became a bystander in the family. He did not say much and lived with the verbal abuse from Natalia.

Eventually Mike decided to bring his sister, her husband, and their family to the United States. This was quite an undertaking. He had to get them jobs, housing, and be financially responsible for them. He bought a house for them and arranged jobs and paid for their passages over here.

Once again I saw how unappreciative they were. After a few months, they wanted a different house. The one purchased for them wasn't good enough. They compared everything to what we had. Twenty years of working meant nothing to them and they wanted it free. Again, *I'm selfish*. These words were the most often used in describing me.

During this time my father-in-law turned to me more and more. I went out to his place at the lake, cleaned, worked the garden, and spent some time with him. He had a big garden with potatoes, tomatoes, squash, and a big grape arbor. My oldest son, Mitch, drove grandpa out to his lake. Mitch loved that old car. Natalia wouldn't go because it wasn't a nice big cottage like we had.

When Vasalie died in 1966 at the age of about seventy-seven, I was already divorced, but I would go up to the hospital and hold his hand. He'd say, "Helen, you're a good woman, but he no good [speaking about Mike]." I will never forget these words because after twenty-five years of doing my best, they were the only really kind words he ever spoke to me.

Natalia died on October 31, 1986, at the age of eighty-six, and so she did live to see many of her grandchildren.

REFLECTION AND INFORMATION
ON SENATOR HUBERT H. HUMPHREY

Without the help of then Senator Hubert H. Humphrey I don't think Natalia would ever have gotten here. He was a strong supporter of the common people and their civil rights. We are very fortunate he was on our side. He became mayor of Minneapolis in 1945 and in 1948 helped Minneapolis enact the nation's first municipal fair employment law. He was a United States senator for Minnesota from 1948 to 1964. In 1964 he became the vice president under Lyndon Johnson. He did run for president in 1968, but lost by a very small margin to Richard Nixon.

Family Life
1955–1965

Helen Age 33 to 43

By this time Mike had built up a good real estate and construction business. I never knew how much money he made as he said it was none of my business. The children and I still lived on a very tight budget. He would pay for a tutor for Bob because he thought that would make his son normal. He was not satisfied to just control me; he wanted to control everyone he worked with. My friends could only be people who did business with him or bought a house from him. My best friend had another contractor build her home and after that Mike forbade me to see her again. I still didn't know how to fight back. If it wasn't for my children, I would have given up. They gave me the will to live and go on. I could not be weak and have my children survive.

PRIOR LAKE CABIN

In the 1950s we bought a cabin on Prior Lake, about thirty miles from South St. Paul, and I spent the summers there with the children. This came about mainly because the doctors said Bob would benefit from being able to be by the water and swim. He was doing better, but still struggling. Meanwhile, I was trying to handle taking care of the lake cabin, our house in town, and transport the kids around. This sounds nice, but I still felt trapped and as if I had no way out. I could not have any friends unless they bought a house from Mike's real estate company. I belonged to a club that was made up of the mothers of my children's school friends. When they came to the lake we had so much fun, but at 3:00 P.M. they would all leave before Mike came home. Mike did nothing except inspect things to see that they were up to his standards.

VACATIONS

Our vacations were always taken when and where Mike wanted them. It was never a family decision. After Christmas it was a slow time in the real estate and construction business so we always left for vacation on December 26th. The children were not very happy about this. They had just gotten all these new toys and wanted to spend their vacation playing with the toys and seeing their friends. They were told how lucky they were that their father would take them any place.

Packing for four children and two adults with everything going in boxes was a challenge. We needed a variety of clothing because we would be driving through three seasons of weather: first warm winter clothes, then clothes for a little milder climate, and finally clothes for when it was hot. We tried to make the best of the driving trip by playing games, and having lunch, which was sandwiches and milk, at the side of the road. There were no fast food places like we have today, and we certainly could not use Mike's money to eat in a sit down restaurants. This kind of dining out was not something he would pay for. He was very selective about what we spent money on. We ate cereal in our motel rooms for breakfast. Mike was great for getting rolls for us to eat. We stayed in the cheapest motels we could find in Florida. Often he parked the car, a Cadillac because he liked nice cars, a block or two away, and I would walk and get the motel rate, so the motel manager would not see the kind of car we were driving. Mike would go to the beach whenever it was warm so we could swim, and he took us to see all the sights such as Cypress Gardens and Sea World. I think he went more for himself than for the children. He would take lots of pictures to show his friends.

After Bob and Barb were a little older and Mike was tired of going to Florida, he made arrangements with a tour guide in Mexico City, Mexico, to meet us and take us and then drive us to Acapulco, about 250 miles away. At this time we just had the two younger children traveling with us, so it was a little easier. This was around 1960 and Mexico was not the tourist destination that it is now, so this was quite an experience. These vacations were more fun as the children grew older.

We had only one vacation without the children and that was to Phoenix, Arizona, and then up to Las Vegas, Nevada, for a few days. It was nice, but when I was to be constantly reminded of how lucky I was to be married to this wonderful man, it really put a damper on the fun.

THE BEGINNING OF VOLUNTEER WORK

After my children were all in school I became active in PTA. I held every office from president to treasurer. I kept a good rapport with the teachers. I did this so I could help my children and the school, but even more, I felt that people appreciated what I did. I was also active with the cerebral palsy organization and our church. Mike was never part of this, but that was all right. These outside activities were good for me, and I felt better about myself. I could see a little sunshine out of the black tunnel.

MY BROTHERS AND PARENTS

My brothers and I were fortunate because, unlike many of the children in the orphanage, after we left the school we kept in contact with each other and our parents. It took other children most of their lives to get reconnected with the rest of the family and for some children, they never found their birth family.

One night, not too long after I got married, my youngest brother Dick, age sixteen, appeared at my door. He had run away from the orphanage. I enrolled him in school so he could get an education. He slept in the basement of our house. When the cops came to find out if he was there I told them no. They knew he was with me but thankfully didn't do anything about it. He joined the navy when he was seventeen. It was 1942. He later married and had seven children and many grandchildren. He had a successful career as a land surveyor and currently lives in the state of Washington.

My oldest brother, Harold, couldn't accept institutional living at all and ran away every time he could. He had the scars of the beatings on his back to show for it until the day he died. Every child takes to institutional living in their own way, and he could not deal with it. Harold worked at Swift's Meat Packing Plant and got married and had a daughter, but that marriage never worked out. In his later years he lived with his daughter and she was wonderful to him. He passed away in 1993.

Donald, being crippled, spent the school year at Gillette State Hospital for Crippled Children, in St. Paul. They did a great job with his rehabilitation. He would spend his summers at the orphanage. I remember him telling me a story about where I slept after I was born. He said I was really small and there was no crib or bed for me so my parents put me in a shoe box and put the shoe box in a drawer. He went to live with our mom after he got out of orphanage. Eventually he got married and moved to Kankakee, Illinois, where he bought a radio station and had a successful career there. He had two children. Donald lived until 1991.

Jack, the second youngest brother, grew up with my mother's parents. He went in the air force and made that his career. He met an unfortunate end when he was murdered on the base when he was only thirty-six, in 1961. They never found out who killed him.

My brothers and I never talked about the orphanage or why our parents left us. None of my brothers ever returned to the orphanage.

After my parents divorced, my mom went to Hurley, Wisconsin, and remarried. She got divorced again and moved to the West Coast, living with sisters along the way, and eventually met her third husband and lived in Portland. My mother gave me the impression that my father was worthless. She never said anything about putting us kids away in an orphanage, and she certainly did not apologize for it. I never brought up the topic because I wanted a mother and I didn't care what she did. I was afraid if I brought it up, she would leave me again. In 1959, she moved to St. Paul and lived with my brother Harold. There was never a mention to any of us as to why we were given away.

Shortly before she died, my mother and I went to a nondenomination spiritual retreat in Green Lake, Wisconsin. Those who attended had an opportunity to talk with others in a group about whatever was on their mind and get feedback from the group. I talked with the minister who was in my mother's group, and he told me that my mom finally broke down and talked with other people about what it was like to give up the kids, but I never heard what she said. She had a heart attack in 1965 and died at age sixty-five. I was by her side and saw the mother I had always looked for taken away from me. I am fortunate that I did have her in my life for those five years before she died. My kids got to know her. She was a fun loving person, and I miss her.

I kept in touch with my father over the years. He also remarried two more times. His last wife was not very understanding of his seizures and would beat him when he had them. When my father got ill with cancer I went to Huron, South Dakota, and was by his side when he died at age fifty-seven in 1955. I remember my dad telling me, "Helen, don't do anything for me. I never did anything for you. Don't say anything bad about your mother. It takes two and she never had a chance." I didn't see it that way. At the time he died I thought he had left us and that my mother wanted us. It was not until many years later I learned that the opposite was true.

END OF THE MARRIAGE 1965

HELEN AGE 43

The decade of the 1960s was a very colorful time in history. When I look back now I wonder how much all the change that was happening in the country and the world finally motivated me to get out of my marriage. During this decade John F. Kennedy was elected president and assassinated, Martin Luther King was changing our view of civil rights and was assassinated, and there were civil rights riots. We sent a man into orbit around the world, the Twist was the new dance, the Beatles and Woodstock were changing our music, the war in Vietnam started, and we had beehive hair, hot pants, mini skirts, hippies, and psychedelic clothes. If ever there was a climate that fostered independence, it was then. The decade was crammed with peace, love, war, and excitement.

I remember Mike started doing more business traveling alone, and he told me he was going out to California to see a guy who had worked for him. When I called his hotel room, he was never there. I would question him when he came home, which he didn't like. Sometimes when he was in town he would have real estate appointments in the evening and did not come home until midnight. It always seemed odd to me that he was selling houses at midnight. I finally confronted one of the people he was supposed to be meeting with them and found out he was lying.

The final pieces came together after he made a trip to San Francisco, California. When he came home I picked him up the airport, and when I was putting the luggage away, I found a beer opener with the name of a hotel. The next time he left town I called the hotel and pretended to be one of the kids and told them it was an emergency and I had to talk with my father. The hotel said he had checked out the day before. I asked if both my mother and father checked out and was told yes. Then I called a hotel in Las Vegas and found out that a couple had been there a day or two before. He always stayed at the same hotel, so that made tracking him down easy. I did the same thing telling the hotel there was an emergency and I needed to get hold of the couple. Now I knew for sure that he was seeing someone.

After my investigation, I called the lawyer and sheriff and said I wanted him out of the house. I knew that once he left he could never come back because if he did, he would have beaten me unmercifully. When Mike got back to town the sheriff told him to come home and pick up his things and to leave the house and never return. Mike was a very proud man, and I knew he would never forgive me for bringing in the sheriff and making him look bad. It was hard. He made me out to be the bitch and said I was the one who did everything wrong. Fortunately there were many people in town who knew us and understood what he had been doing. There were questions about his business dealings, and he made the mistake of bragging about his relationships with other women to many people in the community. Perhaps the final straw for the Romanian community was that the woman he was seeing was a very close relative by marriage. Mike got little sympathy from the people who knew him. We separated for nine months until the divorce settlement was final. When I finally got the divorce papers, it was Christmas Eve, 1965. The attorney brought me the signed papers and said," Helen, this is long overdue. I'm taking it and putting a red ribbon it. Why did you wait so long? What you are going to do?"

LIFE AS AN INDEPENDENT WOMAN— 1965 • HELEN, AGE 43

What am I going to do? Mitch had been in the navy and was out in the working world, Bette was married and a mother and had a life of own life, Bob would soon be graduating from high school and going in the navy, and Barb was fourteen and living with me. I was free to do whatever I wanted but freedom came with a price and many questions. How was I going pay my bills? Could I find a job? I had not worked for decades and had no formal training to do anything. Could I make new friends? Most of the people I knew were Romanian. Who would pick me up if I fell, both emotionally and physically? I was really starting over.

RETREATS—1965 • HELEN, AGE 43

Shortly after my divorce, my minister, Dave Kachel, who had been very supportive of me during my divorce, suggested I go to a retreat in Green Lake, Wisconsin, about 250 miles from South St. Paul. He said there were going to be about five hundred people at this non-denominational spiritual growth retreat. This was going to be hard for me because I was not still used to being out on my own in large groups, but I trusted him and I said I would go.

My first experience at the retreat was a bad one. I went to be a part a group of people who practiced laying on of hands. How I looked was important to me so before this retreat I had my hair done and there were a lot of bobby pins holding my curls together. As the people kept laying their hands on my head I'm thinking, "Get your hands off my head. My bobby pins are coming out!" I guess I did not have very realistic expectations of what was going to happen at the retreat. I had expected the dove of peace to come and light on my shoulder and be illuminated and feel loved. This wasn't working and I ran out. I was very upset. I still carried with me the baggage of abuse, abandonment, depression, and had no light in the tunnel.

As I was leaving the group I met Lee Whiston, a minister, and he came to sit with me. I started telling him how I felt; I cried and got all my feelings out. He said, "God loves you." I said if he did, why was my life the way it was? He said I had to turn more of my life over to God. He told me I couldn't handle all this alone, and I needed to ask God for help. I did not realize it until much later, but when I asked God for help he did send it almost immediately, just not the way I expected. I met Lee and his wife, Irma, at three future retreats and did learn that God loved me and that I did not have to face everything alone.

MAKING A NEW LIFE

One of my friends had a business selling sample clothes, and I was a perfect fit for modeling them. This eventually led to me meeting a clothing distributor and they hired me to be a model in their fashion shows, which they held two or three times a year when the new clothing lines came out. One of the large hotels in town held the event and there were many other distributors there. I was coming out of a room and heard this voice, "Helen, what are you doing here?" and there was Mr. Hertz from the family I had worked for thirty years before. I had kept in touch with them off and on over the years but didn't expect to see him at this event. He teased me about working for a competing dress company. Modeling was great for my ego and a good start to what I needed to help me feel better about myself. I also got to keep, or could purchase at reduced prices, beautiful clothes. This was opening the door for a whole new life for me. I did this for about three years.

About this same time, a friend of mine was working for a trucking company and they were looking for some office help. I said I could do it. I took care of the routes of the drivers and did general office work. At first I didn't have much confidence in myself, but I loved the job and started to come out of the dark tunnel. The people I worked for made me feel good about myself. I was a typical divorcee and a bit of a flirt and enjoyed being in an environment with all these men who treated me kind and nice. They respected me. In time I became more confident and self assured. I could dress in nice clothes, wear makeup, and the real me started to come out. Life was entirely different. After four years they closed that division and I got laid off.

Hansel and Helen

I started going to the Golden Steer, a nice bar and restaurant close to South St. Paul, and I made new friends. For the first time in my life I had my own friends, and I could do things that I wanted to do and there was no one to tell me how to live my life. I was having a good time. After being hidden for years, my natural extroverted and outgoing personality started to come out. My life was definitely looking up.

SORORITY

Not very long after my divorce I became involved with a philanthropic sorority. I was asked to talk about Bob and his physical challenges and my life at a meeting of the Epsilon Sigma Alpha sorority. They were amazed by what I had gone through to get Bob well. I was asked to join the sorority and I did. In 1970, I was nominated for the DIANA Award. It is the Distinguished International Award for Noble Achievement, and it is presented to a woman who has given outstanding service to the community. There were a total of five women nominated from Minnesota. I am very proud of my statue of the Greek goddess Diana. Here is what they wrote about me in their February 1970, newsletter:

> "To provide a complete summary of Helen's self-giving for others and the benefits received would be impossible to do within this article. However, a few examples may provide some insight.
>
> "Helen has worked through many groups to bring help to others. Through many hours involved in the preparation and serving of dinners and telethons, she has supported the work of United Cerebral Palsy. In countless hours invested in committees and group meetings she has given dedicated leadership to the Parent Teachers Association in our city, seeking to improve our schools and the relationship between home and school. Through her service on the Board of Deaconesses of her church, she was instrumental in

establishing a daily meal service bringing one hot meal a day into homes where the mother was hospitalized or bed-ridden. Through her work with the youth council she has battled for the youth of our community in finding a wholesome place for gatherings and recreation.

"But perhaps even more important has been her 'one on one' relationships: befriending the Mormon missionaries and providing them a 'Mom' and a 'home' away from home; welcoming into her home for weekends delinquent girls from the House of Good Shepherd; keeping in contact with some of the lonely old timers in our city, from Europe, who still have problems with the English language; making and selling scarf holders to sew into coats to provide $50.00 Christmas shopping money for a lady with Cerebral Palsy. The list goes on and on. A kind word, a helping hand, and even the wisdom to provide a good scolding when someone has been wallowing in self-pity, have all been a part of Helen's ministry to others."

That pretty much sums up how I had been spending my time for the first five years after getting divorced. I could never have done any of these things when I was married. Mike did not believe in helping others unless they were Romanians. Doing volunteer work has been a constant part of my life and is very rewarding to me.

REFLECTION AND INFORMATION

After our divorce, Mike dated several other women but for one reason or another, none of them worked out for him and he never remarried. His business continued to grow, and for many years he stayed in touch with his children and even attended family birthdays and holiday events. He would be there along with me and that worked out fine. The last decade of his life his health started to deteriorate and, whether it was from over medication, physical illness, or mental illness, he became a recluse. He stopped coming to family events and went into his office at night or early in the morning when no one was there. He died a multi-millionaire, but alone in his small apartment in 1998.

I have come a long way since my divorce but my insecurities still show up from time to time, especially at night. For example, I start thinking about how my kids reacted when I got divorced. I remember back and wonder why my children did not do much to help me around the house after I got divorced. They were always around for cookies or for their birthday presents. Mitch came over every day for a beer, but never ever did he mow the lawn, shovel snow, or do anything to help around the house and yard. My neighbor did the shoveling. I felt as if my kids divorced me when I divorced their father. Mike made it especially difficult for Barb. His view was she could not love both parents, and he wanted her to choose between us. Barb was only fourteen, and Mike put her in a terrible position of choosing between father or mother.

Another example is when Bob went in the service, which was about the same time as the divorce, and I wanted to see him off at the airport. He said, "Mom, don't bother." Bob said the apron strings had to be severed. Another example that I fretted about for thirty years was that Bob and Fay did not ask me to his college graduation, but they did ask his dad. I thought, "Once again I am left out." I finally asked Fay about it. It turned out Bob was not even living in the college town anymore and no one went to his graduation. I guess I should have asked about it sooner. When I ask myself the question now, "Why did my kids divorce me?" the answer I get is, "They were asserting their independence and starting their own lives, and it had very little to do with the divorce."

DOMESTIC VIOLENCE

Much can be said about the changes in our society and how it views domestic violence and abuse. In 1940 people just did not talk about it and there was no safe place to go. Now it is recognized as a serious problem and you can talk about it. Minnesota was one of the leaders in providing safe houses where a mother and her children can go to escape abuse. Today there are shelters, safe houses, community advocacy programs, criminal justice intervention projects, 24-hour crisis lines, and much more. These resources and organizations, both public and private, can help both the victim and the abuser and are making a difference. Those who give their financial support, volunteer time, and work so hard to keep these programs going are very special people. Many women and children owe them their lives. I know my life would have been so different if they had existed when I was being abused.

There are other organizations that focus on education, research, and changing the policies and systems. Janet Hagberg, living in the Twin Cities, has played an important role in starting an international organization called Silent Witness. The mission of Silent Witness is to "Promote peace, healing, and responsibility in adult relationships in order to eliminate domestic murders in the United States by the year 2010." Their vision is to "Promote successful community-based domestic violence reduction efforts in order to reach zero domestic murders by 2010."

ABANDONED, ABUSED, AND NEGLECTED CHILDREN

The reasons for children being abandoned, neglected, and abused are no different today than they were in 1886, when the orphanage opened. Parents still have economic problems, accidents, become ill, are mentally unfit, fall victim to substance abuse, go to prison, or die. Fortunately what has changed is society's ways of caring for these children. There are many public, private, county, state, national, and international organizations that help provide safe and loving homes for children. Foster homes and adoption are two ways we are trying to give homes to children. Our society continues to try to find the best ways to deal with the children and their families.

Mary Jo Copeland, in the Twin Cites, is another example of how one person can make a difference. The nonprofit organization she started, Sharing and Caring Hands, is working to make a home for children with the establishment of Gift of Mary Children's Home. The mission of Gift of Mary Children's Home is to "provide a safe and loving, nurturing environment for children where they can grow emotionally, physically, spiritually, and academically toward the goal of being happy, well-adjusted, self-sufficient, responsible adults."

There are some who think group residential facilities should not be considered as a solution. I grew up in one and although it certainly wasn't perfect, it did give me a much better life than I would have had on the streets of St. Paul. Our society should have an open mind to looking at all possible solutions. No matter what the answer is, there would be good orphanages and group homes and bad ones just as there are good foster homes, good adoptive parents, and bad ones. The important thing is to work for a better future for these children and their families.

My Light at the End of the Tunnel
1966–1986

Helen Age 44 to 64

The light at the end of my tunnel, the miracle God sent me, the answer to my prayers came in the form of a man named Ed Bowers. I met him about the same time I was going through my divorce. I was at a friend's house making Christmas pine cone trees, and he came to the door delivering a package from Dayton's department store, where he worked as a truck driver. He sat on the steps and had a cup of coffee with us, and we started talking. I had seen him a few times when he delivered packages to my house, and I thought how nice and good looking he was. He was always so courteous, polite, thoughtful, and kind.

Ed was divorced after a twenty-five year marriage, and I was separated after a twenty-five year marriage. He called my friend that night and told her he was going to marry me someday. She said, "You are crazy. When Helen gets out of this marriage she won't ever think about getting married again." It was not very long before I started dating Ed and found that there was at least one man who could love me just as I am with no strings attached. Eventually he moved into my home. When I would go out with my girl friends to the Golden Steer, he would say "just drive safely." When I got home he had dinner ready.

My next job, around 1970, was when a neighbor of mine was opening an insurance office, and he asked me if I could help him get the office set up. The branch manager was coming in from Madison, Wisconsin, and I was introduced to him. He said to my boss, "What's she doing here? She should be out in the field selling insurance. She is a natural." One thing led to another, and I soon found myself in Madison attending insurance school. A middle-aged woman in an insurance class was almost unheard of at that time. I remember my instructor making a comment about having a woman in class, and I asked him afterward what he meant. He told me he didn't like women in classes; insurance was a man's profession. Training went on for quite a few months and each time we met we had to tell how much insurance we had been selling. Guess what, every time I made more money than the men did. I did get my insurance license and found that not only did I like this job, I was successful at it. I also felt I was doing something good for people.

Sometimes at night if I was going to a bad part of town Ed would go with me and just wait in the car until I was done. I was awful with directions, and with all the delivery experience that Ed had, he knew the Twin Cities' streets well. He would write out detailed instructions on how to get to my next insurance call and when I still got lost and called him, he patiently told me where I made my wrong turn. He never, ever, made me feel dumb.

The insurance business was heart breaking because when I had to pay out an insurance policy, I went in person to give the family a check. The worst ones were when a child died, but even then I felt I was doing something good and giving the family a small bright spot in the middle of their grief. Sometimes the business was really fun. I won a ten-day trip to Hawaii with all expenses paid. I was really out of the tunnel now. I was successful and loved meeting people, but eventually the driving, evening insurance calls, and the pressure of the business started to take its toll on me. I started getting terrible migraine headaches and my doctor encouraged me to find something else to do, so after four years I quit that job.

I worked as a receptionist at a bank, and I loved it. It was my responsibility to hand out free gifts to people who opened new accounts. What a great job. I worked there for ten years and retired from there the first time when I was sixty-five. Not too long after I retired they asked me to come back, and this time I worked until I was seventy.

In all the years Ed and I have been together he has never cut me down or said anything unkind to me and has always been supportive of whatever I wanted to do.

He is everything that Mike was not. Do we have disagreements or fights? Very rarely, and if we do, they last only a short time. Over the years we have both learned that there are so few things that are worth getting upset about. We never go to bed angry. Ed is famous for his chocolate chip cookies and just recently his "Grandpa's Chocolate Chip Cookie" recipe was published in the *100th Anniversary NMB [National Mutual Benefit] Cookbook* published by the National Mutual Benefit Company.

Some people have said that Ed seems too good to be true, but he is sincerely caring, polite, protective, and unbelievably devoted to me. I am so lucky. He is the one who turned my tunnel of darkness into a never ending tunnel of perfect light. In his first marriage he did not have the opportunity to share all the love and affection in his heart, and so, he says, he just saved it up all those years so he could give it to me.

Things have not always been perfect with the children in his family or mine. Ed has two children who, unfortunately, choose their mother over their dad. Ed's son, Jeff, could never accept the fact that we were living together and not married. It took many years for Barb to accept Ed. Perhaps that was the control Mike had over her and it made her feel she had to choose her dad and could not allow space for Ed. My children didn't know what it was like to receive this kind of love and affection from a man or see it given to their mother. They had never been around a man who would hold the door open for me or stand when I entered a room or hold my chair out for me, much less give me a kiss on the cheek.

I was happy the way we were, just living together, and I didn't think there was anything to gain by being married. For a few years we lived in the house that Mike and I had. Finally, I told Ed we needed something that was ours together, and so I sold my house and we both bought the townhouse we live in and it is truly our house. For quite a few years we also owned a mobile home on a lake in Pine City, Minnesota, and spent many weekends with new friends and our family. Ed loves to fish, and he and my little grandson Jeff had some wonderful times taking the pontoon out and catching fish.

After Ed retired from Dayton's and I retired from the bank, we both volunteered at the Children's Museum in St. Paul and tutored children in fifth grade at the local school. We even won an Outstanding Volunteer Award from Medica [a local HMO] and were on stage at the Minnesota state fair with many other volunteers to receive our award. We volunteered for about five years. At the same time, we started taking ceramic courses together and spending time at arthritis swimming classes two times a week. We really are very busy people. When we stopped the volunteer work, we found we had time on our hands, so we both went to work part time for Sam's Club giving out food samples. We really enjoyed doing this.

Finally, after twenty years, we decided to get married. Well, to be really honest, Ed would have married me any time, but I was happy with the way things were. My independence and having things that were mine was so important to me. Why did I change my mind? We each have our own bank account and a joint account. It wasn't financial. I got tired of trying to explain our living arrangement. It would feel good to say "this is my husband" instead of boyfriend, significant other, or partner. We came to a point in our spiritual life that it was the right thing to do. I thought maybe my kids would feel better about it and that Ed's son would like it better. In the beginning it didn't work out that way with his son, but now their relationship seems to be improving and they go out for lunch on a regular basis. I was sixty-four and Ed was sixty-two when I finally accepted his marriage proposal.

MARRIAGE AND A NEW LIFE— FEBRUARY 14, 1986 • HELEN AGE 64

We are romantics and got married on February 14, 1986. Don't tell me I wasn't scared! For decades I didn't know men like Ed existed, let alone one who would marry an orphan and treat her like a queen. The day of the wedding Bette told me to make sure I was ready at 4:00 P.M. She said someone would pick us up. We were really surprised when a man in a chauffer uniform picked us up in his limo. We were married at North Presbyterian Church in North St. Paul, Minnesota. Each of my children was in the wedding. Mitch was the best man, Bette the maid of honor, and Barb and Bob were attendants. Our good friend Rev. Dave Kachel came out of retirement for the ceremony along with Rev. Cook, the minister of the church. We had a beautiful reception in the party room of Bette's condo in the Twin Cities and celebrated with many of our good friends and family. After that we left for our honeymoon in Ft. Meyers,

Florida, where we stayed with Bette in her Florida condo. She took us sight seeing around Florida. It could not have been a more perfect wedding and honeymoon. I would not say that I am Cinderella, but I feel like her, and Ed certainly is my Prince Charming. Sometimes fairy tales do come true.

Ed and Helen 1986

After almost forty years together he is still the most wonderful man in the world. He has taken care of me in sickness and in health. I have had eight back surgeries and spent considerable time in a wheelchair and have had hundreds of therapy and doctor appointments that he takes me to. For one operation I was in Rochester, Minnesota, for five weeks. He rented an apartment across the street and was at the hospital at least twelve hours a day. After that surgery I was in a wheelchair for two years. That was a very difficult time for me. I was used to being independent. During that time he did the washing, ironing, cooking, and cleaning, and continues to do the majority of the work around the house. There are still times when I get very sad and cry, but Ed just takes me in his arms and holds me until I feel better. I don't know what I would do without him. He is the light in my life now.

Recently Ed has needed several surgeries for his shoulder and knees, and I have had the privilege of being able to take care of him. I think after my divorce God took a look at me and thought *Helen, you have had enough bad things happen to you in your life so from now on it will be the time for happiness.*

YOUNG CHILDREN

My older son, Mitch, went into the navy around 1959 after he graduated from high school. He wasn't interested in going

on to school so it was really the best thing for him. While in the navy he realized how important an education was going to be. He went on to college and graduated from Hamline University in St. Paul, Minnesota, and then he went to work at Control Data Corporation, which was one of the pioneering supercomputer firms. He worked there for about four years, and then his father became ill and insisted that he come to work in his real estate and insurance business.

Children 1952

That was beginning of Mitch's downfall. His father constantly controlled him. Mitch could never please him. He would get depressed and started to drink.

In 1976 he married Lyn, a woman with a son age three and a daughter age five. Before too long Mitch adopted the two children. They had several happy years together, but later got divorced because of his drinking.

I still keep in touch with Lyn. Fortunately she has been able to rebuild her life and is happily married again.

Mitch never got over the divorce and his health started to fail. He isolated himself in his apartment with his computer for company. He stopped communicating with any of his siblings for a number of years. Even though I rarely saw him, we talked frequently by email and on the phone. We were able to put the bad days behind us and stayed on good terms. He died on July 1, 2002, just a few weeks short of his sixty-first birthday. Even though he was too sick to know, all of his brothers and sisters and children were with him before he died.

Bette, my older daughter had to grow up too fast. Her childhood was cut short by having to do the housework and take on the responsibilities of an adult when she was but a child. She helped with the cooking and took care of her brother Bob when she was only ten years old. She never complained. I was really strict with her and expected perfection. She married Dale Schenian when she was sixteen years old. They first lived in a home her father helped them buy on the street behind us. She had no problem being a good wife, mother, and housekeeper. She gave me my first grandson, Michael, on Thanksgiving Day, 1959. I was a grandmother at age forty. Even though she and her husband, Dale, were very young when they were married, and like most couples, have had their ups and downs, they are now doing well.

Bob had the most challenges to overcome and made a full recovery. He was able to completely retrain his mind and body. When you meet him you would never guess what he had to go through when he was a child. After he graduated from high school he went on to join the navy at age seventeen and was sent to Vietnam. He was in the navy for three years and was done before he was twenty-one. They called that the "Kiddy Cruise." He does not talk about Vietnam much, but I know it was not a pleasant experience for him. After the navy he went on to graduate from Mankato State College, where he met Fay Randen, and got a business degree in finance. He is a network engineer at a large company. Bob was the lucky one. Unlike Mitch, he got out of his father's office before it destroyed him.

My younger daughter, Barb, is still my baby. She was able to lead a fairly normal life, except when I was in the hospital with my nervous breakdown. Barb got her own apartment when she was eighteen years old. After that we drifted apart for a few years, but still kept in contact. In 1984, she gave me a grandson, Jeffrey. She raised Jeff on her own, but maintains a good relationship with Jeff's father. I have helped her as much as I could.

My kids are made of tough stuff. I have watched them work through the rough spots in their lives. Mitch with his dad, kids, and wife; Bob with a house that was hit by a tornado and another one that was hit by lightening; Bette who

Barb, Bob, Mitch and Bette 1980s

had her new home burn a few years ago; Barb who has been a single parent. The kids all get along with each other and, though not close in the respect that they see each other all the time, I know they are there for each other.

Life Out of the Tunnel
1986–2005
Helen Age 64–83

Revisiting the Orphanage

Unlike my brothers, I have returned to the orphanage several times. I took my children there in the 1950s because I wanted them to see what had influenced my life so much. I know it is hard for them to understand what that life was like. How do I explain that the reason I was such a perfectionist housekeeper was because when I was growing up I had to be on my hands and knees scrubbing this huge dining room floor at the orphanage? When things were perfect at the orphanage I did not get punished.

The orphanage grounds are beautiful and many of the buildings still exist. The buildings got a second life from 1945 to 1970 when the facility provided nationally recognized academic and vocational programs for educable retarded persons. From 1970 to 1974 the facility was unused until the Owatonna City Council petitioned the State Department of Administration and the Legislature to buy the seventy-four-acre campus. The buildings are used for city and community offices. But that is not the end of the orphanage story.

The children who were raised in the orphanage, their families, and anyone with an interest in history owe so much to Harvey Ronglien, State Schooler (that is what we called ourselves), and his wife, Maxine. Harvey and Maxine have been tireless in keeping the memory of the school alive. When the orphanage was built, it was the best way known to provide for orphans, dependent, and neglected children. Since then many things have changed and now there are other solutions to this problem, but society should never forget what that life was like.

With lots of enthusiasm from Harvey and many individual and business sponsors, the old site has a very nice orphanage museum within the old Administration Building and beautiful grounds. In 1993, a dream came true for many of us when we placed 151 crosses with names on the graves of children who were buried and forgotten in the cemetery. The inscription on the monument at the cemetery reads *"1888-1942 To the children who rest here may the love you lacked in life now be your reward in heaven. You are remembered."* I guess it's much like my own little sibling who has been forgotten. At that time we also put up a statue to pay tribute to all of the

Kids monument dedicated in 1993

"State School Kids." In 1994, Lutheran Brotherhood placed a guardian angel on a corner of the cemetery to watch over it. In the spring of 2001, a memorial boardwalk was started; in 2002, a documentary video was made; in 2004, a beautiful new rock garden with a waterfall was built to replace the one that was there many years ago; and a memorial to the state school servicemen, who died in World War II, was put up on a new flag pole in the Plaza.

I hope you will go to the Orphanage Museum and learn much more about what this life was like.

About ten years ago I gave the invocation at the first State Public School Reunion. Letters were sent to every State Schooler inviting them back. It is hard to describe how I felt when I looked out and saw all the faces of State Schoolers who had been like my brothers and sisters. There were over four hundred of us. They came from England, North Dakota, California, Texas, and many other states. There were families like the four brothers who had never seen each other, reunited for the first time. We talked about things that happened while we were growing up. It has been difficult to share our memories with others who did not share our experiences. This sharing was a highlight of getting together. We passed the microphone around and remembered what our life was like so many years ago. The boys remembered the hard work and stern punishment. The girls remembered the nursery and cleaning and working in the kitchen. Since then there have been four reunions, and I have been to all but one. Each year there are fewer and fewer of us as we pass on or are confined to nursing homes and wheelchairs and can't make the trip.

In the summer of 2004, Bob and Fay drove Ed, my grandson Jeff, and me down to see the grounds. That was a very special day for me. I never dreamed my eighteen-year-old grandson would have an interest in seeing this. I was surprised when he asked if he could go with us. By this time Fay and I had been working on this book, and I could tell it was a special day for her also.

TV INTERVIEWS

It's impossible to predict what events in your life will have an impact on you or where the journey will take you. I mentioned earlier that there was a video about the orphanage. In 2002, the Minnesota Historical Society worked with Harvey, Maxine, and others to make a documentary of the orphanage called *The Children Remember*. The documentary film is a composite of stories told by those who were there. For some, the orphanage was a circle of hell; for others, a safe haven. I was one of fifteen people interviewed and appeared in the film. What an incredible experience that was. There was a big premiere for the people involved in the production of the video and their families at the Historical Society, and it has been shown on several public television stations. It won the American Association for State and Local History award. It has also been shown at many other events around the Midwest. I am most excited to say that at age eighty I became a film star.

A few months after the documentary came out; I was interviewed by Judy Skeie-Voss, Production Supervisor for On Location TV 19. This is the local origination production department of the Ramsey/Washington Suburban Cable Commission in St. Paul, Minnesota, and they seek out and create community related programming. She wanted to do a segment on TV that told more about my life and experiences in the orphanage and as an abused woman. While telling her my story I mentioned Ed, the light in my life, and our Valentine Day marriage. She was intrigued and wanted to know more. A few months later she asked for another interview with Ed and me and wanted us to tell her our love story. Our story was shown as a special throughout the months of February in 2004 and 2005 on our local cable channel. Now I am a TV star. One thing I have learned is that I have to be prepared for anything and grab the opportunities when they come.

MY BIRTHDAY PARTY

One of my happiest memories is my eightieth birthday party in October 2002. When I was a child we never celebrated a birthday and so a party on that day has always had a special significance to me. After much planning, my children arranged a dinner party at a nice supper club and invited eighty of my family and friends. Bette and Barb sent out invitations, planned the meal, and made all the other arrangements. I was so excited and then the night before I fell and broke my nose. I could not let a small thing like that set me back. I just put on a little extra make up and no one noticed a thing.

Fay made posters that showed photos of my life and ran old movies of our family growing up. She put flyers on all the tables that told about events in my life and what had happened in the world during my life. That was a big hit.

Bob was a fantastic master of ceremonies. He told a wonderful story that included all the people who have touched my life. There were many happy, teary-eyed people in the audience by the time he was done. I felt so loved and important, like a queen, and I was flying on a cloud of love. The party and all my family and friends made me feel I could forget the bad things and that I would never go back in the tunnel again. It was after this party that Fay started talking with me about getting my story in writing. She has been persistent.

A SPECIAL GIFT

When Fay and I were working on the book we got talking about the fact that I might not have gone back to get my high school diploma. I had forgotten all about it. She did not. She said it took her almost six months and many emails telling the school about me but her persistence paid off. On Mother's Day 2004, she gave me my framed high school diploma from Central High School in St. Paul, sixty-five years after I attended the school. What a special gift. When she gets an idea, she rolls with it.

THE LAST LITTLE ORPHAN

One more adventure still awaited me. I told Fay I had no interest in finding out about my sibling who died when I was a child. She had all kinds of questions. Wasn't I curious about the baby? Didn't I want to see if the baby had a grave stone and what its name was and when it lived and died? I told her no. I did not want to know. I had my brothers and that was all I needed. Fay is an only child and I think it really bothered her that the baby was forgotten and that no one cared. I thought the subject was closed and forgot it but she did not.

She had nothing to work on except my parents' names, where they might have lived, and a four-year range of time when the baby might have been born. There was no baby name, no date of birth, and no date of death. For all we knew, no baby existed. She started by trying to find the church. I told her it was a Presbyterian church but there was no church like that in Frederic, Wisconsin. She went to the Internet and found a minister and called him to ask about the cemetery. Fortunately, there was only one cemetery and one funeral home and she got the name of the funeral director. They had no records at the funeral home that went back that far. The funeral home director could tell her nothing except the name of the sexton who took care of the cemetery. She tried to find the woman through phone information but had no luck. Since Frederic is a small town, and Fay grew up in a small town, she figured everyone knew each other. She just asked the operator for anyone with the same last name as the sexton and in two phone calls had her person. She found out from the sexton that there were people with the name Hoover buried in the cemetery and that a burial plot was being paid for starting about the time when the baby might have died. It was winter and the graves were covered with snow so we could not easily visit the cemetery.

Around this time I broke my foot and was in a wheelchair or on crutches, so she said nothing to me for many months until she knew I could get to the cemetery. Finally, in the summer of 2004, she asked me again if I wasn't curious about the baby. I must have mellowed out over the winter, and after she told me what she had done, I agreed to go to Frederic to see what we would find. Bob and Fay took Ed and me on a beautiful summer afternoon drive to Frederic. We met the sexton and drove to the cemetery. We found the headstones of other relatives of mine buried there, but no stone for a baby. I could tell Fay was disappointed. She asked the sexton where the county death records were kept, and she told us that they could be found in the county seat court house which was on the way home.

We quite easily found the first set of death records. We looked in the record book for the name of anyone who died with the last name of Hoover in the early 1920s and found five names. I was prepared to find one baby but certainly not five and there were both girls' and boys' names listed. I did not want to have a sister at this point in my life. The next step was to match the death records with death certificates and learn who the parents were, age of the person who died, and the cause of death. I was nervous and did not know if I wanted to find out any more. I've lived all these years without knowing, but there was no turning back now. Fay kept looking, and we found that the rumor I had heard for eighty years was true. I did have another brother and his name was Clifford Thomas. He was born March 23, 1921, in Frederic, Wisconsin, and died thirteen days later on April 3, 1921. My father gave the information that was on the death certificate and all it said under the cause of death was that his mother found him deceased. When I heard the baby's name I was not surprised. I must have heard it before. I'm glad we went. I know for Fay it means that she found "the last little orphan," and just like the 151 children in the orphanage cemetery, this forgotten child now had a name. We never did find out where little Clifford was buried.

EPILOGUE
2005

Being abandoned, growing up in an orphanage, and being a victim of abuse are woven into who I am and took me into my dark tunnel. While the orphanage provided an environment that met our physical needs, they could not provide love to the 10,000 plus children they were trying to help. These children often grew to become adults who did not know how to love or be loved and many had low self esteem. I wanted to be loved and approved of. I would have to say that neither Mike nor I had any positive role models to teach us what a happy marriage should be like or how to be good parents. I needed love and approval, and he had no way to provide it to me. After all these years, the pain he caused me has lessened. I find that now I feel sorry for him because he never learned to love or be loved.

In the beginning, my children were what kept me going. Having them get sick was so hard and made me feel like a failure and helpless. I wanted their lives to be normal. It took so much out of me to get them well, but they needed me. Their illnesses didn't stop me from being afraid that I would do something wrong and then they would stop loving me. I wanted my kids to be happy, and I think they are. I tell them I love them every time I talk to them. I grew strong when I had to be strong for them and that has helped me through my own illnesses. Having God send me Ed showed me what love and hope were about and has provided me the light in the tunnel.

I have put much of the painful past behind me. When I first started this book I couldn't write down my memories without crying. Although I had shared much of my story with others, there were still things that happened to me that I could not talk about. I would lay awake at night and have all these memories go through my mind. With the help and support from Fay I could start to express those hidden memories and my feelings. I found that when I could talk about it with her, I started to heal.

It hasn't been all bad. My life journey has been in steps and missteps. I can hardly remember the times I was sick and in the wheelchair. I always tell people that I have had a good life. Sure, things could have been different along the way. Whatever it was that happened, I got over it or I got through it. I learned that God or a higher power only gives you as much as you can handle, but you have to ask for help. I can't live my life hating and bearing grudges. People need to understand that no matter what the circumstances of childhood and your life are, you don't give up.

Through it all I did pretty well. I can look back and say, "Wow that was quite a mountain to climb but I made it." I hope I have made Ed and my children happy. I can tell you that I have been out of the tunnel for many years and my life is filled with light from many places. I want to tell all the women out there that no matter what adverse circumstances you have, you can overcome them if you believe in yourself and God. Love yourself and tell your children and others in your life that you love them.

Helen and Ed 2005

ADDITIONAL RESOURCES

- Award winning video/DVD *The Children Remember: Life at the State Public School for Dependent and Neglected Children.* 87-minute documentary film. 2002. The documentary was funded in part by the Minnesota Historical Society's Grants-in-Aid Program, and by corporate and individual donations. The video or DVD is available from the Orphanage Museum web site or call 507-444-4321.

- Orphanage Museum web site— http://www.orphanagemuseum.com

- Minnesota Historical Society Orphanage Records– 651-296-2143—http://www.mnhs.org/genealogy/ family/genieguide/owatonna_school.htm.

- Mary Jo Copeland's Sharing & Caring Hands— http://www.sharingandcaringhands.org

- NCADV—National Coalition Against Domestic Violence—http://www.ncadv.org

- MNCB–Minnesota Coalition for Battered Women—http://www.mcbw.org/

- The Day One Center—http://www.dayonecenter.org

- Silent Witness–http://www.silentwitness.net

- *While the Locust Slept*—book by Native American orphan Peter (Jim) Razor Published by the Minnesota Historical Society Press, St. Paul, 2001

- *Patty's Journey*–book by orphan Donna Scott Norling with afterward by Priscilla Ferguson Clement Published by University of Minnesota Press, Minneapolis, 1996

- *No Tears Allowed*—book by orphan Eva Carlson Jensen, available from Sandy Dinse, 2002

REFERENCES

- Epsilon Sigma Alpha, philanthropic network, newsletter February, 1970

- Freidman, Morgan S. *The Inflation Calculator.* http://www.westegg.com/inflation/

- McMurry, Martha, *Turn of the Century, Minnesota Population in 1900 and Today,* Minnesota Planning State Demographic Center, November 1999

- Minnesota Historical Society, Helen Bowers orphanage records from the Owatonna State School

- Minnesota Historical Society. http://www.mnhs.org/library/tips/history_topics/42humphrey.html

- Minneapolis Morning Tribune, December 19, 1958

- Minnesota State Public School Orphanage Museum newsletters

- *Owatonna's Thursday Post* July and August 1996
- *The Children Remember: Life at the State Public School for Dependent and Neglected Children,* documentary video, 2002